THE DISCIPLING DILEMMA

Flavil R. Yeakley, Jr., Editor

Howard W. Norton
Don E. Vinzant Gene Vinzant

THE DISCIPLING DILEMMA

A STUDY OF THE DISCIPLING MOVEMENT AMONG CHURCHES OF CHRIST

Edited by Flavil R. Yeakley, Jr.

Flavil R. Yeakley, Jr.
Howard W. Norton
Don E. Vinzant
Gene Vinzant

Gospel Advocate Co.
P. O. Box 150
Nashville, TN 37202

THE DISCIPLING DILEMMA

Published by Gospel Advocate Co.
P. O. Box 150
Nashville, TN 37202

ISBN 0-89225-311-8

CONTENTS

PART I

Church Growth Research Concerning the Discipling Movement Among Churches of Christ

By Flavil R. Yeakley, Jr.

PART II

The Impact of the Discipling Movement On Mission Work Done by the Churches of Christ

By Howard W. Norton

PART III

Historical Roots of the Discipling Movement Among Churches of Christ

By Don Vinzant

PART IV

A Reference Guide to the Discipling Movement Among Churches of Christ

By Gene Vinzant

PART I

CHURCH GROWTH RESEARCH CONCERNING THE DISCIPLING MOVEMENT AMONG CHURCHES OF CHRIST

by Flavil R. Yeakley, Jr.

ABOUT THE AUTHOR

Flavil R. Yeakley, Jr. has served as the director of the Church Growth Institute at Abilene Christian University since 1984. He was chairman of the speech communication program at the University of Tulsa from 1974 through 1984. Prior to that, he spent over 25 years in full-time local church work as a gospel preacher.

He is the author of *Why Churches Grow, Church Leadership and Organization*, several booklets and tracts, and numerous articles.

He is a member of the North American Society for Church Growth, the Association of Statisticians of American Religious Bodies, the Religious Speech Communication Association, and the Association for Psychological Type.

He received his B.A. degree in psychology from the University of Houston in 1970, his M.A. degree in speech communication from the University of Houston in 1972, and his Ph.D. degree in speech communication from the University of Illinois in 1975.

CHAPTER

1

THE DISCIPLING MOVEMENT: A MIXED BLESSING

The discipling movement has appeared in several religious groups under various labels. Several denominations have experienced growth as a result of the discipling movement in various places throughout the world. Those same denominations, however, have been troubled by the doctrines and practices associated with this movement.

The word "discipling" is used in this movement to mean much more than making converts. It is used primarily to describe a system of intense training and close personal supervision of the Christians being discipled. Disciples are regarded as being superior to mere Christians. Disciples are said to be Christians who have received special training. This training includes much more than mere teaching. There is an intense one-on-one relationship between the discipler and the Christian being discipled. The discipler gives detailed personal guidance to the Christian being discipled. This guidance may include instructions concerning many personal matters of a totally secular nature. The person being discipled is taught to submit to the discipler. Furthermore, the person being discipled is taught to imitate the discipler. Christians being discipled are required to confess their sins to their discipler. Such confession is followed by rebuke, correction, admonition, and prayer. If the person being discipled seems reluctant to confess sins, the discipler asks probing personal questions to elicit the confession.

Discipling is hierarchical. There is a clear distinction between the discipler and the person being discipled. A Christian might have many peer relationships, but only one person is that Christian's discipler. That discipler is the person who must be imitated and obeyed. After a Christian has been discipled for a while, that Christian is expected to start discipling others. The result is a pyramid of relationships that resembles a multi-level marketing system. In various denominations where the discipling movement has appeared, the typical pattern has been for the founding pastor of a church to be at the top of the pyramid. That founding pastor disciples a small group of other pastors. Each of them, in turn, disciples a small group of lay leaders. The lay leaders then disciple members one step lower in the pyramid. That hierarchical system continues through as many steps as may be needed as the discipling movement spreads. The growth of the discipling network typically goes beyond one local congregation to include many other congregations established by the parent group.

The result is a pyramid of relationships that resembles a multi-level marketing system.

This description of discipling, of course, does not perfectly fit every group that has ever been a part of the discipling movement. This composite description, however, is very close to each of the groups that has been a part of this movement. The focus of this study is on one particular manifestation of this movement: the discipling movement among churches of Christ. There is general agreement among those inside and outside this movement that the Boston Church of Christ is the leader of this movement today. That congregation is the primary focus of this study.

Some Comments About Labels

For the benefit of any readers who are not familiar with this group known as "churches of Christ," we need to begin with some comments about various terms. If conditions were ideal, it would not be necessary to use labels that set one group of Christians apart from other Christians. Conditions, however, are not ideal. Christians are not perfect. The church has experienced numerous divisions throughout its history. Discussion of these divisions is not possible without the use of some labels. Such labels could be used in a judgmental way. In this study these labels are used only to describe a social reality with all judgment being left up to God.

The term "churches of Christ" is used throughout Christendom with reference to the spiritual fellowship of all the saved. Pioneers of America's Restoration Movement—such men as Thomas and Alexander Campbell, Barton W. Stone, and many others—used this term with reference to their congregations to emphasize their purpose of being Christians only.

Three heirs of the Restoration Movement are listed in *Churches and Church Membership in the United States 1980.*[1] The smallest of these groups has the most liberal theology. They are known as the "Christian Church (Disciples of Christ)." They are listed as having 4,324 congregations with 817,650 members in the United States. A more conservative fellowship that is somewhat larger is listed as "Christian Churches and Churches of Christ" because some of their congregations use one designation and some the other. This group is listed as having 5,293 congregations with 929,650 members in the United States. The largest and most conservative of these three groups is know as "churches of Christ." They are listed as having 12,719 congregations with 1,239,612 members in the United States. This fellowship differs from the group known as "Christian Churches and Churches of Christ" in two significant ways. Churches of Christ believe that what is done in congregational worship must be specifically authorized in New Testament teaching. Because of this, they do not use instrumental music in worship. The group known as "Christian Churches and Churches of Christ" uses instrumental music in worship because they believe that Christians can do anything in worship that is not specifically forbidden in New Testament teaching.

Churches of Christ typically use the plural word "churches" rather than the singular form to emphasize their independence as local congregations with no central denominational organization or headquarters. They often use the lower case "c" in the word "churches" to emphasize their purpose of identifying with the fellowship of all the saved without forming any denominational organization. The Boston Church of Christ and other churches of Christ identified with the discipling movement grew out of this most conservative of the Restoration Movement fellowships.

Several different terms have been used to describe the discipling movement among churches of Christ. Some supporters have used the term "restoring churches."[2] Others call them "multiplying churches."[3] These self-serving terms are judgmental toward other churches of Christ and thus have not been accepted by most critics of this movement. Some critics have called this the "total commitment movement." Supporters have not generally accepted this term because it focuses on just one part of what this movement is about. Most critics have been reluctant to use this term because it implies that the critics are opposed to total commitment.

The most common terms which critics of this movement have employed use some form of the word "Crossroads." They talk about the "Crossroads movement," "Crossroads churches," the "Crossroads philosophy," or "Crossroadsism." These terms have been used because of the key role the Crossroads Church of Christ in Gainesville, Florida, played in the development of this movement. This discipling movement was first introduced into churches of Christ by Charles H. (Chuck) Lucas in this congregation.

Under the leadership of Chuck Lucas, the Crossroads Church of Christ achieved rapid growth through its campus ministry at the University of Florida. They began training people for similar ministries elsewhere. Soon other churches of Christ wanted campus ministers who had been trained at Crossroads. However, most of these churches that employed Crossroads-trained campus ministers eventually divided into discipling churches and churches that oppose this approach.

. . . most of these churches that employed Crossroads-trained campus ministers eventually divided into discipling churches and churches that oppose this approach.

Terms that identify all discipling churches with the Crossroads congregation are not especially useful. Supporters have never accepted these terms. Furthermore, leadership of this movement has now shifted away from Crossroads. Lucas left the congregation in 1985 and is no longer the leader of this movement. The Boston Church of Christ is now the leading congregation among the discipling churches.

Terms such as "discipling churches" or the "discipling movement" seem to be the only terms acceptable both to the supporters and the critics of this movement. The discipling churches use the term "discipling" in reference to a particular form of evangelism and a particular way of teaching, guiding, and influencing people after they have become Christians. If other churches of Christ use the term "discipling" at all, they generally limit its application to evangelism. The idea of discipling someone who is already a disciple is foreign to their understanding about how this term should be used. Other churches of Christ practice evangelism, but not in the same way the discipling churches do. They also provide teaching, guidance, and influence for those who have already become Christians, but not in the way the discipling churches do. For this reason, they do not mind *not* being called "discipling churches."

The Boston Church of Christ

Supporters and critics generally agree that the Boston Church of Christ is now the leader of the discipling movement among churches of Christ. The rapid growth of this congregation has been amazing. Indeed, that growth is the most persuasive argument in favor of the discipling approach.

The Boston Church of Christ was originally known as the Lexington Church of Christ since it began in Lexington, Massachusetts, a suburb of Boston. The congregation had existed for several years without achieving much growth. Membership in the spring of 1979 was around 40. In June of that year, they employed a Crossroads-trained minister and things have never been the same since.

Kip McKean was converted at the Crossroads Church of Christ while he was a student at the University of Florida. He was trained by Chuck Lucas. After leaving Gainesville, McKean attempted to develop discipling ministries in several congregations. These efforts met strenous opposition. In June of 1979, Kip and his wife, Elena, moved to Lexington, Massachusetts, to work with the small congregation in that Boston suburb. They brought with them about 10 young people who were being trained for service in discipling ministries. Half of the members who were in the Lexington Church of Christ when McKean moved there eventually left—most because of their opposition to the discipling approach. That left a very small work force, but that small group achieved a remarkable record of rapid growth.

There were 68 baptisms in the last six months of 1979. Then there were 170 baptisms in 1980, 250 baptisms in 1981, 365 baptisms in 1982, 402 baptisms in 1983, 594 baptisms in 1984, 703 baptisms in 1985, and 818 baptisms in 1986. In the first seven-and-one-half years of McKean's ministry with this congregation, they baptized 3,370 people. It now appears that they will baptize between 900 and 1,000 in 1987. That would mean a total of well over 4,000 baptisms in just eight-and-one-half years.

Growth was so rapid that the Lexington Church of Christ soon was too large for its building. They rented the building of the Arlington Baptist Church until they grew too large for that meeting place. They started meeting in the Boston Opera House. When they outgrew that facility, they started meeting in the Boston Gardens where the Boston Celtics play basketball and the Boston Bruins play ice hockey. Early in 1987, they were averaging around 2,500 in attendance on Sunday mornings. Virtually all the members were attending one of the 62 house church meetings conducted each Wednesday evening and at least one of the 260 Bible Talks conducted at various locations throughout the Boston area each week.

Early in his ministry with the Lexington/Boston Church of Christ, McKean decided that the discipling approach could not be developed properly in existing churches. There were divisions in almost all of the congregations where the Crossroads-trained ministers introduced this approach. Furthermore, these ministers found it difficult to keep new converts faithful in congregations where many of the members did not appear (to these ministers) to be totally committed, really spiritual, or seriously involved in evangelism. McKean decided that he would not train workers and send them into existing congregations the way Chuck Lucas had done at Crossroads. Instead, he decided to concentrate on planting new churches.

The story of the new churches planted by the Boston Church of Christ is even more dramatic than the story of rapid growth in Boston. In June of 1982, they planted a new congregation in Chicago. By the end of 1986, that congregation had baptized 567 people. In July of 1982, the Boston church started a new congregation in London. By the end of 1986, that church had baptized 627 people. In June of 1983, the Boston church sent a team to plant a new church in New York. By the end of 1986, that church had baptized 649 people. The Providence, Rhode Island, House Church of the Boston congregation became a separate congregation in June of 1985. By the end of 1986, they had baptized 83 people. In August of 1985, the congregation in Boston sent a team to begin a new church in Toronto, Canada. By the end of 1986, they had baptized 159 people. In 1986, the Boston church planted four new congregations. In June they sent a team to Johannesburg. By the end of that year they had baptized 33 people. In August they sent a team to Paris. By the end of the year they had baptized 10 people. In October they sent teams to Stockholm and Bombay. By the end of the year, the Stockholm church had baptized nine and the Bombay church had baptized two.

This is a total, counting the baptisms in the Boston church, of 5,509 baptisms in just seven-and-one-half years. The figures by the end of 1987 will be even more impressive. No other congregation among churches of

Christ today has a record that comes close to this. Indeed, one would be hard pressed to find a similar record of growth from such a small beginning in such a short time in any religious group anywhere in the world today. This amazing record of growth should not be minimized.

An even more amazing chapter is being added to this story. Several of the churches started by the Boston Church of Christ have already started new mission works on their own and many more are planned for the near future. Now other discipling churches that grew out of the work at Crossroads have started following the example of the Boston church. Instead of training workers and sending them into existing congregations, they are planting new churches. In the last section of this book, Gene Vinzant identifies all these discipling churches that have been started or that are now being planned.

Concerns of Other Churches of Christ

Other churches of Christ view the amazing growth of the discipling churches with mixed emotions. They rejoice because of the number of people being baptized. They are pleased to see the emphasis on mission work. They are concerned, however, because of the previous divisions and the problems they have seen in the discipling movement. They fear that the rapid expansion of this movement will mean the spread of these problems throughout the world.

There are several reasons for the concern which other churches of Christ feel in regard to the rapid growth of the discipling movement. They fear that the people they are seeking to reach with the gospel may be confused by the presence of two different churches of Christ that are similar in some ways, yet quite different in other ways. They fear that the people they are seeking to reach may react negatively to the methods of the discipling churches and that this negative reaction may close the door to evangelism by all churches of Christ. They also fear that when discipling churches are started in areas where other churches of Christ already exist, the new discipling churches may recruit members from the existing congregations. Their main concern, however, comes from their belief that the discipling churches are teaching and practicing things that they should not be teaching and practicing. They fear that the doctrines and practices of the discipling churches are damaging people psychologically and spiritually.

The Hierarchy of Discipling Churches

The gap that separates discipling churches from other churches of Christ has recently grown much wider. An ecclesiastical hierarchy is developing among the discipling churches. Other congregations that grew out of the work of the Crossroads church are being taken over by the Boston church. This takeover is not just an informal matter of influence, although that is the way Al Baird and Steve Johnson represented it at a forum at Freed-Hardeman College on October 10, 1987.[4] They said that the argument was just about words. Other churches of Christ, however, do not just object to the words used to describe this takeover process. What they object to is what the discipling churches admit they are doing.

An ecclesiastical hierarchy is developing among the discipling churches.

In this new system that is emerging, there is a new organizational structure in which one congregation officially assumes the oversight of another congregation. The evangelists and elders in one congregation control, direct, and exercise authority over other congregations. This hierarchy extends through several levels so that the Boston church has direct or indirect control over a large network of congregations throughout the world. The plan is for the Boston church to exercise direct control over several key congregations known as "pillar churches" with the pillar churches controlling "capitol city churches," the capitol city churches controlling "small city churches," and the small city churches controlling "countryside churches."[5]

The pillar churches in the United States have been identified and boundaries have been drawn for their "spheres of influence." Seven such pillar churches in the United States have been identified thus far. These are the discipling congregations in Atlanta, Chicago, Denver, New York, Providence, San Diego, and San Francisco. In addition, 17 pillar churches outside the United States have been assigned various foreign spheres of influence. The Boston Church of Christ is not listed as a pillar church. It is at the top of the pyramid, directing the 24 pillar churches.[6]

This new ecclesiastical hierarchy is a clear departure from the doctrine of congregational autonomy taught by churches of Christ since the early days of the Restoration Movement. That is not really being denied. What is being denied is the validity of the congregational autonomy doctrine as it has been taught and understood among churches of Christ.

The doctrine of congregational autonomy is based on the New Testament pattern. That pattern includes independent local congregations. It does not authorize any level of church organization above that of the local congregation. It does not authorize one congregation to exercise authority over another congregation. The departure from this pattern and the development of an ecclesiastical hierarchy was one of the major factors in the apostasy that turned the church of the first century into the Roman Catholic Church by the sixth century.

The doctrine of congregational autonomy has been

very important in the history of the Restoration Movement. Churches of Christ and Christian Churches divided in the late 1800s. One of the issues involved in that division was a Missionary Society that functioned as a level of church organization above the level of the local congregations. In the early 1900s, there was a division between the Christian Church (Disciples of Christ) and a more conservative and independent Christian Church. There were many issues relating to theological liberalism that led to that division. The final break, in the 1950s, came over a "restructure" plan that shifted control from the local congregations to a central denominational organization.

Churches of Christ cooperate with one another, but the typical practice is to exercise great care to avoid any appearance of anything that would violate the autonomy of a local congregation. When a congregatin sends out a missionary to start a new congregation, for example, the supporting congregation has oversight of his work, but they do not claim to have oversight of the congregation established by that missionary. They might offer advice to a new mission congregation if asked to do so, but they would never exercise authority over that congregation. They would never attempt to direct or control that church. They would regard any such action as a violation of congregational autonomy. The recent development of an ecclesiastical hierarchy among the discipling churches is a clear break with their roots in the heritage of the Restoration Movement. What they are doing now is a clear violation of congregational autonomy.

In November of 1986, the Boston Church of Christ had this statement in its bulletin: "We are excited to announce that the Elders of the Boston congregation have assumed oversight of the Kingston Church of Christ, a two-year-old mission effort originally planted by the Miami-Gables congregation."[7] In a pattern that was soon to be repeated throughout the United States, the preacher for the Kingston congregation was taken to Boston for further training and the Boston church sent in its own preacher.

One week later the Boston Church of Christ announced another takeover. In 1985, the Crossroads church had targeted Vienna, Austria, for a new church planting. The sponsorship of this mission effort was shifted from Crossroads to Boston and the leader of that mission team was moved to Boston for further training.[8]

On April 29, 1987, the Gateway Church of Christ in St. Louis was taken under the Boston umbrella. The Shandon Church of Christ in Columbia, South Carolina, started that congregation almost one year earlier. After the takeover, one of the preachers went to Boston and the other to Chicago for further training. The Chicago Church of Christ, one of the pillar churches directed by the Boston church, assumed oversight of the St. Louis congregation. They sent in their own preachers to direct the work. They changed the name of the congregation to the "St. Louis Church of Christ." They described this as a "replanting" of the work in that city. Ever since then they have referred to the date of the replanting as the beginning of the work in St. Louis.[9]

In July of 1987, the Boston church announced a takeover attempt that was not completely successful. Kip McKean said,

> At the invitation of Sam Laing and the other evangelists of the Atlanta Highlands congregation, the Elders, the Lindos and I sought to inspire an evangelistic revival in the congregation. However, due to opposition from within the congregation to such Biblical principles as the authority of the evangelist, one-on-one discipleship and the calling of every member to evangelism, the Elders and I were asked by these same evangelists to consider planting a new congregation

> where the before-mentioned principles would be taught and practiced.[10]

What happened in Atlanta, according to personal correspondance and telephone conversations with those involved, is that some of the members of the Atlanta Highlands congregation refused to accept the claim that the Boston Church of Christ should have authority over the Atlanta Highlands congregation. This case followed the same pattern seen earlier. Sam Laing moved to Boston for further training. The Boston church sent in its own team, including an evangelist and 15 full-time interns. The Boston church assumed the oversight of the "remnant" which formed this new congregation. Those who wanted to be a part of the new congregation were interviewed to see if they would be acceptable.

Kip McKean said concerning the new congregation, "My vision for the Atlanta congregation is to become the pillar church for the entire Southeastern United States."[11] He then went on to list nine cities where this pillar church would plant new congregations. The pillar church status of the new Atlanta congregation raises the question about the status of the older Crossroads-type congregations in the Southeast. McKean listed eight such churches and said that the Boston church planned to help these congregations while training the Atlanta church so that it would be "more than capable of meeting all their needs."[12]

The next month, the bulletin of the Boston church included a report of another takeover, this one in Berkeley, California. In June, the preacher who started that church—Tom Brown—went to Boston for further training and decided to stay in Boston until he could plant a new discipling church in Los Angeles. The Boston church sent a preacher to initiate what was called the "rebuilding" of the Berkeley congregation. In

August, the Boston church officially began directing the church in Berkeley. On August 2, Tom Brown, Al Baird, and Kip McKean outlined for the congregation the plans for the "reconstruction." Notice that all three of these men were members of the Boston church—not the Berkeley church. There were three elements in the reconstruction plan the Boston church imposed on the Berkeley church.

First, they had to move from Berkeley to downtown San Francisco and become "the San Francisco Church of Christ." Second, all their evangelists and women's counselors had to resign and become interns. McKean explained that this was required so that "when they are appointed in the future, they will be recognized in Boston as well as in our church plantings, such as in Bombay or New York."[13] He went on to say, "I foresee this to help form a uniform standard of recognition throughout the multiplying ministries."[14] The third requirement in this reconstruction is that "every individual who desires to be a member of the new San Francisco congregation will need to count the cost of being a disciple."[15] If this requirement means what it did in Atlanta, the members will have to be interviewed to see if they will be acceptable.

Another takeover was announced recently in the bulletin of the Mission Church of Christ in San Diego. They said that they had agreed to follow the Boston church "with a true disciple's heart." As insiders in the discipling movement know, that language means total submission without question. Once the Mission church submitted to Boston, they were recognized as a pillar church and given oversight over California, Arizona, New Mexico, and Texas. One of the congregations that now reports to the Mission church is the East Valley congregation in Phoenix. I recently interviewed a preacher who had been invited to move to Phoenix as an "elder intern." He declined the offer when he learned that the East Valley congregation is directed by the Mission church in San Diego and that they are directed by the Boston church.

A similar situation now exists with the Denver Church of Christ—a discipling church started recently by the Crossroads congregation. The Denver church has now joined the Boston hierarchy as a pillar church. The Boulder church has been told that it must merge with the Denver church. Other discipling churches in that area are expected to work under the oversight of the Denver church.

There was a very revealing statement in the Boston bulletin in a note at the end of a two-page spread listing all the church plantings that have taken place and that are planned by the Boston church and by other discipling churches:

> As discussed at the Leadership Meeting at the 1986 Boston World Missions Seminar, here are the mutually agreed upon guidelines for targeting a city:
> 1. Prayer and fasting.
> 2. A man (of intern status) who is qualified and commended by the brothers.
> 3. Contact churches in the targeted city.
> 4. If another congregation has a planting in that nation, no targeting of those cities. Exception: if the initially planted church agrees, then there may be another city targeted from another congregation.[16]

The third and fourth rules are incompatible unless one understands that two different kinds of churches are being discussed. The third rule means that the discipling churches have to let other churches of Christ know that they are going to plant a new church in their city. That is all. No cooperation is contemplated. They can move in next door to a congregation not identified with the discipling movement and all they have to do is to notify them of their plans. The fourth rule, however, is talking about discipling churches only. In that case, they cannot even send a mission team into the same nation where another discipling church has already been planted—at least not without their permission.

This statement clearly shows that in the thinking of those who lead the discipling movement, discipling churches now constitute a totally separate fellowship from the fellowship of other churches of Christ. This attitude is reflected even more clearly in their frequent use of the term "remnant" to describe themselves. They see themselves as a remnant sent by God to call the faithful out of the "mainline" churches. Still more recent developments suggest that the circle is being drawn even tighter. The older discipling churches started as a result of the work at Crossroads are being excluded if they refuse to join the ecclesiastical hierarchy headed by the Boston church.

. . . in the thinking of those who lead the discipling movement, discipling churches now constitute a totally separate fellowship from the fellowship of other churches of Christ.

Some of the leaders of the original discipling movement that came from the Crossroads congregation are now resisting the takeover attempts by the Boston church. John C. Whitehead of the Crossroads church recently wrote a booklet, "Stop, Look, Listen," in which he warns against the Boston takeover effort. The Miami-Gables congregation has been resisting the Boston takeover attempts. Now, the Boston church plans to start a new congregation in Miami.[16] What is happening now, however, is only the logical extension of what was taught at a different level earlier throughout the discipling movement. If every Christian must be discipled in a hierarchical discipling system within a local congregation, why not insist that every congregation must be discipled in a hierarchical discipling system that puts one congregation in a position of authority over another? There is as little Bible authority for one of these ideas as for the other.

Now, however, the Boston church has started teaching a doctrine of authority that goes far beyond what was taught earlier in the discipling movement. They are teaching that Hebrews 13:17 applies to matters of opinion. They are claiming that this verse gives authority in matters of opinion to evangelists and elders, zone leaders, house church leaders, Bible Talk leaders, and disciplers. Al Baird told members of the Atlanta Highlands congregation that it would be a sin to refuse to obey the instructions of a discipler—even in a matter of opinion with no biblical justification at all because of the claim that God has placed that discipler over that Christian. Some observers believe that this is what was being practiced all along in the discipling movement, but they did not admit it or try to defend it until recently. What is happening now, however, is that discipling with its requirement of imitation and unconditional submission is being extended to congregations. The Boston church is discipling its pillar churches. They are discipling other churches. Eventually this Boston-led hierarchy is supposed to extend throughout the world.

Dilemmas

In writing this material, I have had to point out some very serious problems with the discipling approach. That may make some people think that I regard the discipling churches as being totally wrong and other churches of Christ as being perfect. This is not what I believe. I see much good in the discipling churches. I also see many failures among other churches of Christ. But when I discuss the good things I see in the discipling churches and the failures among other churches of Christ, some may think that I totally endorse everything about the discipling movement. This is not at all what I intend to communicate.

These dilemmas, however, simply involve the discussion of the issue, not the issue itself. The discipling dilemma is far more serious. It involves the question of how we can help others become more and more like Jesus Christ without making them over in our own image and thus changing them in ways that have nothing at all to do with Christianity.

A central element in the debate over the discipling movement as it has appeared in various denominations throughout the world has been the charge that this movement involves a control that is foreign to the spirit of Christianity. Critics of this movement charge that its leaders are making members over after their own image. According to these critics, members are controlled in such a way that their personalities are changed to conform to the group norm. These critics argue that such personality changes are destructive psychologically and spiritually.

. . . members are controlled in such a way that their personalities are changed to conform to the group norm.

The discipling dilemma offers two equally unacceptable alternatives. One extreme is to insist on changing people at all costs—even at the cost of their personhood, autonomy, and uniqueness. The opposite extreme is to avoid such unhealthy changes by not helping people change at all. The way to escape from this dilemma is to recognize that there is a third alternative. We can help people change in ways that are uniquely Christian, but avoid making them over after our own image. A related dilemma offers churches of Christ two equally unacceptable alternatives. One is to accept the discipling approach totally in spite of some very serious problems. The other is to reject everything about this approach in spite of its many strong points.

After years of careful observation, I have come to the conclusion that the discipling churches are right in many of the things they do. They emphasize evangelism and get virtually all of their members involved in evangelism at some level. They have a very effective small group approach to evangelism. They are careful to make sure that prospective converts are thoroughly taught before they baptize them. They place a great emphasis on mission work and send some of their best people to the mission fields. They are conservative in doctrine. They spend most of their money to support the preaching of the gospel and little on paying for a church building. They are active in confronting sin in the lives of their members. They get their members into personal relationships that could encourage spiritual growth if used properly. They are baptizing a large number of people. They have a low drop-out rate. These strong points are important and they must not be ignored. By way of contrast, years of careful observation have forced me to the conclusion that many other churches of Christ are failing in these very areas where the discipling churches are succeeding.

There is, however, a very serious problem in the discipling churches that is not generally found in other churches of Christ. The next chapter presents the results of some research conducted in the Boston Church of Christ. A psychological test was administered to over 900 members of that congregation. Results of that study provide convincing evidence of an unhealthy pressure toward conformity in the Boston Church of Christ. It is changing the personalities of its members in unhealthy ways. Later in this book, you will find several follow-up studies done after the original research in Boston. Results of these studies provide compelling proof that the personality changes are being produced by the discipling methods employed by that church. Various comparison group studies show that these personality changes are not generally found in other churches of Christ or in various mainline denominations—but the very same pattern of personality change is observed in studies of various sects that are highly manipulative.

Discipling churches have some very serious problems in spite of the fact that they are doing a lot that is right. Other churches of Christ do not typically have the same problems, but there are many ways in which they are failing to do what they ought to do. Churches of Christ would face a terrible dilemma if these were the only two options. Fortunately, each congregation of the churches of Christ is independent. All members are expected to study the Bible for themselves and reach their own conclusions regarding matters of faith and doctrine. No individual member and no local congregation has to choose sides and accept one or the other of these two equally undesirable alternatives. There is a third alternative. Churches of Christ can correct all their many failings, do everything good that the discipling churches are doing, but avoid the errors that are producing the psychological manipulation.

Churches of Christ can correct all their many failings, do everything good that the discipling churches are doing, but avoid the errors that are producing the psychological manipulation.

NOTES FOR CHAPTER 1

[1]Bernard Quinn and others, editors, *Churches and Church Membership in the United States 1980* (Atlanta: Glenmary Research Center, 1982).

[2]Robert Nelson, *Understanding the Crossroads Controversy* (Gainesville, Florida: published by the author, 1981).

[3]Milton Jones, *Discipling: The Multiplying Ministry* (Fort Worth: Star Bible & Tract Corp., 1982). Note: while this book seems to be the origin of the term "multiplying churches," the author has an independent ministry not identified with Crossroads, Boston, or any other discipling congregation.

[4]Al Baird, Winford Claiborne, Earl Edwards, and Steve Johnson, "Discipling, Church Growth, and Church Unity," The Third Annual Preachers and Church Workers Forum, Freed-Hardeman College, Henderson, Tennessee, October 10, 1987. Audio Tape.

[5]Bulletin, Boston Church of Christ, January 4, 1987.

[6]Bulletin, Boston Church of Christ, August 30, 1987.

[7]Bulletin, Boston Church of Christ, November 23, 1986.

[8]Bulletin, Boston Chruch of Christ, November 30, 1986.

[9]Bulletin, Chicago Church of Christ, May 3 and July 19, 1987.

[10]Bulletin, Boston Church of Christ, July 26, 1987.

[11]*Ibid.*

[12]*Ibid.*

[13]*Ibid.*

[14]*Ibid.*

[15]*Ibid.*

[16]Bulletin, Boston Church of Christ, January 4, 1987.

[17]Bulletin, Boston Church of Christ, August 30, 1987.

CHAPTER

2

A PSYCHOLOGICAL STUDY

Leaders of the Boston Church of Christ felt that the story of their amazing growth needed to be documented by a qualified church growth researcher. They felt that such a study would be more credible if conducted by someone not identified with the discipling movement. I was given the assignment.

The initial data-gathering stage of this research was conducted during a ten-day visit to the Boston Church of Christ in April of 1985. Leaders of the congregation cooperated fully. I was allowed to sit in on all the leadership meetings. I observed training classes, Bible Talks, Wednesday evening house church meetings, and Sunday morning worship services. I interviewed leaders at all levels in the congregation's organizational structure. I also interviewed over 100 new converts.

The initial stage of the research also included interviews with leaders of other churches of Christ in the Boston area. These interviews focused on relations between their congregations and the Boston Church of Christ. In many of these congregations, there were members who had belonged to the Boston Church of Christ before leaving because of their dissatisfaction with the methods being employed. I questioned these members about their experiences.

Method

Considering all the criticism that has been directed against the Boston Church of Christ, it is remarkable that they were as open as they were in allowing this study. Their openness is strong evidence that they believed that they had nothing to hide. They even permitted me to conduct two different psychological studies. One study involved the two newest converts in each of the 35 house churches that were meeting at that time. Results and implications of that study will be discussed in Chapter 3. The focus of the present chapter is on a much larger psychological study that involved over 900 members of the congregation.

A central element in the criticism that has been directed against the Boston Church of Christ, other discipling churches, and the discipling movement generally has been the charge that these churches employ methods that produce unnatural and unhealthy personality changes. Critics charge that discipling churches tend to make the members over after the image of the group leader, the group norm, or the group ideal. Supporters of the discipling movement deny that any such personality changes are taking place. This, of course, is an empirical question that calls for an empirical answer. There are many mysteries associated with the conversion process that can never be explained scientifically. This question, however, about the presence or absence of personality changes can be answered by the appropriate use of a personality inventory.

The Myers-Briggs Type Indicator

The personality assessment tool used in this study was the Myers-Briggs Type Indicator (MBTI).[1] The MBTI is one of the leading non-psychiatric personality instruments in use today. Unlike tests used to diagnose mental or emotional problems, the MBTI simply indicates normal healthy differences.

The theory behind the MBTI was developed by Carl G. Jung.[2] He observed that there are two essential psychological processes. He called these "perceiving" and "judging." Perceiving means becoming aware. Judging means reaching a conclusion. Jung observed that there are two opposite but equally valuable ways of perceiving. He called these "sensing" and "intuition." He also observed that there are two opposite but equally valuable ways of judging. He called these "thinking" and "feeling." According to Jung, all people use all four of these psychological functions, but not with equal skill. Each person has a preferred way of perceiving—either sensing or intuition. Each person also has a preferred way of judging—either thinking or feeling.

The two ways of perceiving in Jung's theory are quite different. Sensing is the process of becoming aware through the physical senses. Those who prefer this way of perceiving and thus use and develop it more tend to have good contact with reality and the ability to see things exactly as they are. They are able to focus on details that others might not notice. They tend to be very practical. Intuition, on the other hand, is an immediate awareness that comes from memory and associations rather than just from the physical senses. Those who prefer this way of perceiving and thus use and develop it more tend to focus on the big picture more than on details. They are able to see meanings, implications, possibilities, and relationships that others might not notice.

The two ways of judging in Jung's theory are also quite different. Thinking is the process of deciding between the true and the false. It is an objective, logical, critical, analytical process. What Jung called "feeling," on the other hand, is the process of deciding between the valued and the not-valued. It is a subjective, personal, value-oriented process. Feeling is not emotionality. It means making value judgments. Both thinking and feeling are rational processes.

In addition to a preference for one or the other of these two ways of perceiving and one or the other of these two ways of judging, Jung observed that people prefer one or the other of two opposite but equally valuable attitudes. He called these "extraversion" and "introversion." Extraverts use their most fully developed psychological process (sensing, intuition, thinking, or feeling) externally for dealing with the outside world. They deal with their inner world through an auxiliary process—their second most fully developed process. Introverts, on the other hand, use their most fully developed psychological process internally for reflection and deal with the outside world through their auxiliary or second most fully developed process. Extraverts receive energy from the outside world. They get energy from being with people. Introverts may use their energies with people, but they get their energy from within. Everyone extraverts part of the time and introverts part of the time. Jung observed, however, that people have a preference for one or the other of these attitudes.

Isabel Myers and her mother, Kathrine Briggs, elaborated on Jung's writings to develop one other important distinction. They observed that some people prefer to deal with the world through a judging process (either thinking or feeling), while others prefer to deal with the world through a perception process (either sensing or intuition). They noticed that those who prefer to extravert a judging process tend to be highly organized while those who prefer to extravert a perception process tend to be adaptable.

There are 16 different psychological types in Jung's theory as elaborated by Kathrine Briggs and Isabel Myers. All 16 of these types are good. Each has its own unique set of special gifts. There are no bad types—no types that are less desirable than others. When the MBTI identifies a person's preferences and thus a person's psychological type, what is indicated are simply normal healthy differences.

Each of the 16 MBTI types is identified by a four-letter code. The first letter, either "E" or "I," tells whether a person prefers an extraverted or an introverted attitude. The second letter, either "S" or "N," tells whether the person prefers sensing or intuition as a way of perceiving (the letter "N" is used for intuition because the letter "I" was already used for introversion). The third letter of the psychological type code, either "T" or "F," tells whether the person prefers thinking or feeling as a way of judging. The final letter, either "J" or "P," tells whether the person prefers a judging or a perceiving orientation to the outside world—whether the person prefers to deal with the external world through the preferred way of judging (either thinking or feeling) or the preferred way of perceiving (either sensing or intuition).

Changes in Psychological Type Scores

A person's true psychological type is inborn, according to Jung. Some of the preferences can be observed very early in life. A person's true type does not change. Healthy growth, maturation, and development take place within a person's true type. Changes in psychological type do not indicate normal healthy growth. Such changes indicate some pressure in the environment that causes people to deny their true type and try to become like someone else.

It is not healthy to pressure a person to deny his or her true type and become a copy of someone else. Trying to change a person from one psychological type to another is like spanking a child for using the left hand. One does not produce good right-handed people that way. One produces very poor right-handed people who are very frustrated. It would be far better to help the left-handed child develop the skill of using the left hand.

In *Gifts Differing,* as Isabel and Peter Myers were discussing how children develop best, they wrote,

> The finest examples of type development result when children's immediate environment encourages their native capacities. However, when an environment squarely conflicting with their capacities forces children to depend on unnatural processes or attitudes, the result is a falsification of type, which robs its victims of their real selves and makes them into inferior, frustrated copies of other people.[3]

In the MBTI *Manual,* Mary McCaulley said,

> Isabel Myers believed that type preferences were inborn, but that environmental pressures were important in determining the likelihood of optimum type development. . . . Myers wrote that when external influences cause falsification of type, emotional difficulties will follow. It is for this reason that this Manual cautions counselors to check carefully with their clients and with their own observations of the client for evidence of type falsification. This is particularly important in counseling because a goal of treatment is to identify and strengthen the inherent preferences, not to continue the falsification process.[4]

In *Psychological Types,* Carl Jung wrote,

> As a rule, whenever such a falsification of type takes place as a result of external influences, the individual becomes neurotic later. . . . A reversal of type often proves exceedingly harmful to the physiological well-being of the organism, often provoking an acute state of exhaustion.[5]

These quotations should be enough to emphasize the point that changing psychological type scores do not indicate normal healthy development, but may indicate a dangerous falsification of type.

Misguided religious influences could be an environmental influence causing people to deny their true type and try to become a copy of someone else. Martin Buber tells the story of a rabbi who tried all his life to become another Moses, but he never succeeded. Finally he stood before God in judgment and God said, "You are not condemned for your failure to become another Moses; you are condemned for your failure to become yourself."

Christianity, of course, requires one kind of change in personality. Christians are being made over after the image of Jesus Christ. His divine nature, however, is reflected in individuals whose gifts differ. Christian growth does not require falsification of type. Indeed, spiritual growth is hindered by any effort to deny one's true type and become a copy of someone else.

The MBTI can be administered with three different sets of instructions as a way of checking for falsification of type. Such falsification of type would be indicated by changes in psychological type scores. When a family counselor, for example, has reason to suspect that a teenager is being pressured to become a copy of a father or mother, the counselor may have that teenager take the MBTI three times. The first time the instructions are, "Answer the questions the way you think you would have five years ago." The second time the instructions are, "Answer the questions according to the way you think, feel, and act at the present time." The third time the instructions are, "Answer the questions the way you think you will answer them five years from now." If the results indicate that the teenager's psychological type scores are changing and becoming more and more like that of a parent, that result could indicate an unhealthy pressure on that teenager to become a copy of that parent. Such a result would suggest the direction the treatment of that family ought to take.

A similar approach was taken in the study of the Boston Church of Christ. Around 900 members of that congregation took the MBTI. They were asked to answer the questions three times. One time the members were told to answer the questions the way they think they would have before their conversion—or five years ago for the few who had been members that long. The members were also told to answer the questions the way they would at that present time. Finally, they were told to answer the questions the way they think they will answer them after they have been discipled for five more years.

The instructions made it clear that there are no "right" or "wrong" answers and no "good" or "bad" outcomes—just indications of normal healthy differences. The instructions stated clearly that no one was telling them that their answers ought to change. The instructions said that the purpose of the study was simply to find out if there were any changes and, if so, what those changes might indicate.

This kind of group application involving a single psychological instrument is not the approach a clinical psychologist or psychiatrist would take in diagnosing psychological problems of an individual. Several psychological instruments would be used and there would be extensive counseling before any diagnosis would be made if the focus were on an individual. The purpose in this study, however, was not to diagnose psychological problems of any individual. What was being investigated in this research was simply the overall group pattern. The focus was not on any individual, but on the dynamics of the group.

It should also be understood that this was not a

longitudinal study that determined the psychological type of people at three different times. What was indicated was the present psychological type manifested by these people, their *perception* of their past psychological type, and their *perception* of their future psychological type. However, any significant changes in the pattern of these perceptions would indicate some kind of group pressure. A high degree of change and a convergence in a single type would be convincing proof that the Boston Church of Christ has some kind of group dynamic operating that tends to produce conformity to the group norm.

If the supporters of the discipling approach had been correct in their claim that no personality changes were resulting from their methods, this study would have found no statistically significant changes in psychological type scores. That would have cleared the Boston Church of Christ of all charges on this matter. The results would have given them a clean bill of health. For such results to be credible, however, it was essential that the leaders and members of the congregation not be told that changes in psychological type scores do not indicate healthy growth. If they had been given that information and the results showed no statistically significant changes in psychological type scores, critics of the discipling approach would not have accepted the results. They would have claimed that the results were biased by the members knowing in advance that their answers were not supposed to change.

The MBTI forms were passed out in Wednesday evening house church meetings. Some members were busy with retreats that weekend and did not have time to take part in the study. No pressure was put on anyone to take part. However, around two-thirds of the members did take part. There were 835 members who filled out all three forms. A few others filled out only one or two. Among the males, 378 filled out the past form, 402 filled out the present form, and 388 filled out the future form. Among the females, 471 filled out the past form, 478 filled out the present form, and 460 filled out the future form.

Comparative Studies

Before discussing the results of this study in the Boston Church of Christ, it is necessary first to discuss the results of some comparative studies. It would not mean anything to find a pattern of changing psychological type scores in the Boston Church of Christ if similar studies in other churches of Christ produced the same results.

The MBTI was administered to 304 members of churches of Christ that are not a part of the discipling movement. There were 150 females and 154 males in this sample. They were given the same past, present, and future instructions as those used in the study of the Boston Church of Christ. Not a single one of these individuals changed on all four of the MBTI scales or even on three of them. Three people changed on two of the scales and 33 changed on one of the scales. All 36 who showed any change at all in MBTI scores had very low preference scores on the scales involved in the changing scores. This level of change is about what one would expect under these conditions from random test error. The MBTI, after all, is not a perfect indicator. In this comparative study, however, there was no observable pattern in the few changes that took place. Those who changed from Extravert to Introvert, Sensor to Intuitor, Thinker to Feeler, or Judger to Perceiver were balanced by others changing in the opposite direction. The overall distribution did not change.

Another comparative study was completed just recently using this same methodology in studies of 30 members each in five local congregations representing five mainline denominations. These studies were conducted in Baptist, Catholic, Lutheran, Methodist, and Presbyterian churches. Results were the same as those observed in the study of churches of Christ that are not identified with the discipling movement. There were no significant changes in psychological type scores. There was no pattern in the few changes that were observed. Overall distributions did not change.

This is what one would expect since mainline denominations typically recognize and respect individual differences. They value this diversity. They encourage individuals to become what they are uniquely capable of becoming and not mere copies of someone else. This is not the case, however, with certain manipulative sects. It is conformity that they value, not diversity. They tend to make people over after the image of a group leader, the group norm, or what the group regards as the ideal personality. Such pressure to falsify type is one of the reasons for the psychological damage often experienced by their members. They are made to feel guilty for being what they are and inferior for not being what the group wants them to be. As the gap between the real self and the pretended self grows larger and larger, the self esteem of these members sinks lower and lower. They become frustrated and depressed. They may develop serious emotional problems. They may become so dependent on the control exercised by their leaders that they engage in irrational behavior.

With this characteristic of manipulative sects in mind, another comparative study was done. This study used the same past, present, and future instructions with the MBTI to study 30 members each in six local groups representing six manipulative sects. Groups included in this study were: the Church of Scientology, the Hari Krishnas, Maranatha, the Children of God, the Unification Church ("Moonies"), and the Way. Results of this study showed a high level of change in psychological type scores. Results also showed a clear pattern in the observed changes. The past distributions tend to be normal. The present and future distributions deviate increasingly from the normal distribution. The changes in these six groups showed a clear convergence in a single type. In three of the groups, the movement was toward ESFJ. Two moved toward ESTJ. One moved toward ENFJ. One of the reasons the publication of this book has been delayed so long is that this comparative study of manipulative sects was not completed until the summer of 1987.

Results

An appendix at the back of this book discusses all the details of this study with all the appropriate statistical tables. What is discussed here are simply the major conclusions of the study in the Boston Church of Christ.

The first result of this study to be discussed is the observation that *a great majority of the members of the Boston Church of Christ changed psychological type scores in the past, present, and future versions of the MBTI.* Among the 835 individuals who took all three forms of the MBTI, less than five percent showed no change at all and less than seven percent had the same past and future type. Among the rest, a comparison of past and future types showed that almost 20 percent changed on one MBTI scale, 35 percent changed on two, over 26 percent changed on three, and over 12 percent changed on all four scales, thus experiencing a total reversal of type. The mean number of scale changes was 2.18 among the 835 members of the Boston Church of Christ who took all three forms of the MBTI. The present distribution was significantly different from the past distribution. The difference between past and future type distributions was highly significant.

A second result of this study that must be noticed is that *the observed changes in psychological type scores were not random since there was a clear convergence in a single type.* Ten of the 16 types show a steady decline in the percentage who came out as that type in the past, present, and future versions of the MBTI. Three transitional types show an increase from past to present and then a sharp decline in the future outcomes. There were three popular types in this study: ESFJ, ESTJ, and ENFJ. There was a steady increase in the percentage who came out with these three type indications in the past, present, and future results. Percentages are figured separately for males and females since male and female distributions differ on the thinking-feeling scale. In the past, present, and future results, the percentage of males who came out ESFJ went from 2.58 to 26.37 to 54.23 while the percentages for females went from 5.10 to 34.31 to 53.48. ESTJs differ from ESFJs only on the thinking-feeling scale. The percentage of males who scored as ESTJ went from 7.73 to 15.92 to 20.37 while the percentages for females went from 4.67 to 13.81 to 23.04. ENFJs differ from ESFJs only on the sensing-intuition scale. The percentages of males who came out ENFJ went from 1.29 to 4.73 to 14.81 while the percentages for females went from 0.64 to 3.97 to 12.17.

There was a clear pattern of changing from introversion to extraversion, from intuition to sensing, from thinking to feeling, and from perceiving to judging. In the past, present, and future results, the percentage of males with a preference for extraversion went from 33 to 60 to 94 while the percentages for females went from 38 to 64 to 95. The percentage of males who had a preference for sensing perception went from 66 to 78 to 80 while the percentages for females went from 66 to 85 and then to 82. The percentage of males with a preference for feeling judgment went from 41 to 65 to 76 while percentages for females went from 53 to 73 and then to 71. The percentage of males with a preference for a judging orientation went from 37 to 80 to 96 while percentages for females went from 34 to 80 to 95.

Preferences for extraversion, sensing, feeling, and judging tended to remain stable while the opposite preferences for introversion, intuition, thinking, and perceiving tended to change. Among those who started as extraverts, 97 percent remained unchanged, but 95 percent of those who started as introverts changed into extraverts. Among those who started with a preference for sensing perception, 82 percent remain unchanged, but 78 percent of those who started with a preference for intuition changed. Among those who started with a preference for feeling judgment, 72 percent remained unchanged, but 74 percent of those who started with a preference for thinking changed. Among those who started with a preference for a judging orientation, 97 percent remained unchanged, but 95 percent of those who started with a preference for a perceiving orientation changed. There was a highly significant movement away from preferences for introversion, intuition, thinking, and perceiving and toward extraversion, sensing, feeling, and judging.

Those who were the least likely to change were those who already were ESFJs. They averaged only 0.32 changes on the four MBTI scales. Those who were the most likely to change were those who started as the opposite type, INTP. They averaged 3.55 changes on the four scales. There was a strong positive correlation between the number of differences between a type and the ESFJ model, on the one hand, and the mean number of changes on the four MBTI scales on the other hand. The more a person differed from the ESFJ model, the more likely that person was to change on more of the MBTI scales.

What all of this means is that the Boston Church of Christ is producing in its members the very same pattern of unhealthy personality change that is observed in studies of well-known manipulative sects. Whatever they are doing that produces this pattern needs to be changed.

What all of this means is that the Boston Church of Christ is producing in its members the very same pattern of unhealthy personality change that is observed in studies of well-known manipulative sects. Whatever they are doing that produces this pattern needs to be changed.

The six manipulative sects that showed the same pattern as was observed in the study of the Boston Church of Christ are usually called "cults." I do not find that term to be especially useful. Many of the writers who have identified the characteristics of cults reflect an anti-religious, humanistic bias. By most of their definitions, the New Testament church would be called a "cult," churches of Christ today would be called "cults," and most of the conservative denominations would be called "cults." But those six groups that I have chosen to call "manipulative sects" are clearly producing unnatural and unhealthy personality changes.

The data in this study of the Boston Church of Christ do not prove that any certain individual has actually changed his or her personality in an unhealthy way. The data, however, do prove that there is a group dynamic operating in that congregation that influences members to change their personalities to conform to the group norm. To the extent that the members respond to that group pressure, the observed changes in psychological type scores are likely to become (or have already become) actual changes in the personality that is manifested.

This study that was conducted in the Boston Church of Christ has not been conducted in other discipling churches. However, since other discipling churches do the same things that the Boston church does, it is extremely unlikely that similar studies in other discipling churches would find different results.

NOTES FOR CHAPTER 2

[1]Isabel Myers and Kathrine Briggs, *The Myers-Briggs Type Indicator* (Palo Alto, California: Consulting Psychologists Press, 1976).

[2]Carl G. Jung, *Psychological Types* (London: Keegan Paul, 1923).

[3]Isabel Myers and Peter B. Myers, *Gifts Differing* (Palo Alto, California: Consulting Psychologists Press, 1980), p. 189.

[4]Isabel Myers and Mary McCaulley, *The Myers-Briggs Type Indicator Manual* (Palo Alto, California: Consulting Psychologists Press, 1985), p. 64.

[5]Jung, p. 415.

NOTE: The author is thoroughly trained in the use of the MBTI. In 1983 he won the Isabel Briggs Myers Memorial Award for outstanding research in the study of psychological type theory. He served as treasurer of the Association for Psychological Type from 1983 through 1987. He is a member of the faculty of the MBTI training program conducted by the Association for Psychological Type to train professional users of the MBTI. He designed and tested a new self-scoring version of the MBTI now being published by Consulting Psychologists Press. In 1987 the author was elected as the next president of the Association for Psychological Type. Some of his type-related publications are listed below.

"The Relationship between True Type and Reported Type," with Allen L. Hammer, *Journal of Psychological Type* (in press).

"Implications of Communication Style Research for Psychological Type Theory," *Research in Psychological Type* 6 (1983): 1–20.

"Communication Style Preferences and Adjustments as an Approach for Studying Effects of Similarity in Psychological Type," *Reasearch in Psychological Type* 5 (1982):30–48.

In addition to these publications, the author has presented eleven papers at regional and national conferences of the Association for Psychological Type and the Speech Communication Association reporting on his type-related research.

CHAPTER

3

ALTERNATIVE EXPLANATIONS EXAMINED

The facts presented in Chapter 2 (and discussed much more fully in an appendix at the end of this book) demand an explanation.

1. It is a fact that most of the members of the Boston Church of Christ showed a high level of change in psychological type scores.

2. It is a fact that the observed changes presented a clear pattern of convergence in a single type: ESFJ. There was a strong tendency for introverts to become extraverts, for intuitors to become sensors, for thinkers to become feelers, and for perceivers to become judgers.

3. It is a fact that this kind of pattern was not found among other churches of Christ or among members of five mainline denominations, but that it was found in studies of six manipulative sects.

These facts cannot be ignored. They must be explained.

The explanation I offered to the leaders of the Boston Church of Christ was that these observed results indicate a dangerous falsification of type produced by some kind of group pressure. Chapter 4 examines unique doctrines and practices of the discipling churches that may account for the results that were observed in this study. Before considering these things, however, it is necessary first to examine various alternative explanations that have been offered by the leaders of the Boston Church of Christ and various other individuals.

Jesus as an ESFJ

Results of this research were presented to the leaders of the Boston Church of Christ in December of 1985. In that two-day meeting, they rejected my explanation and offered several alternative explanations. The first of these had to do with the psychological type of Jesus. Kip McKean argued that all the Boston Church of Christ is doing is making people over after the image of Jesus Christ. He concluded that this research simply proves that Jesus was an ESFJ.

My response was that one cannot do a personality test on deity. Jesus had all the gifts, not just half of them. ESFJs have four very important gifts. As extraverts, they have a natural ease in dealing with people. As sensors, they have the gift of practicality. As feelers, they are comfortable in the human relations area and are probably sensitive to how other people feel. As judgers, they have the gift of being organized. ESFJs, however, do not have four other gifts that are just as important. Introverts have the gift of concentration, reflection, and ease in dealing with the inner world. Intuitors have the ability to see meanings, relationships, implications, and possibilities. Thinkers have the gift of objective logical analysis. Perceivers have the gift of flexibility. One can argue based on the gospel record that Jesus was an extravert, a sensor, a feeler, and a judger. One can also argue, however, that Jesus was an introvert, an intuitor, a thinker, and a perceiver.

The four psychological processes in Jungian theory may also be viewed as four communication styles. In their book, *From Image to Likeness,* Grant, Thompson, and Clarke suggest that the four gospels were written in the four communication styles.[1] Matthew's gospel is clearly written in thinker style. He emphasizes the things Jesus taught. His gospel is a logical argument that Jesus is the Messiah promised in the Old Testament. Mark's gospel is written in sensor style. Mark tells little of what Jesus said, but emphasizes what Jesus did. Mark's gospel is a gospel of power. It is short, straight to the point, action-oriented, and results-oriented. That is the way good sensors write. The gospel of Luke shows us the human side of Jesus. We learn from Luke how Jesus felt and what He valued. This emphasis is consistent with feeler style. John's gospel is quite different from the synoptic gospels. It is as though he steps back from the details to focus more on the meaning. John presents more of a theological gospel. This style is consistent with the way intuitors write.

Anyone who studies all four of the gospels should be able to identify with Jesus regardless of whether that person is an extravert or an introvert, a sensor or an intuitor, a thinker or a feeler, a judger or a perceiver. All people, regardless of their psychological type, should be able to identify with Jesus. Something is wrong with a proclamation of Jesus if only the ESFJs can identify with Him. Such a result would indicate that one is preaching only half of Jesus. One cannot adequately explain the results observed in the study of the Boston Church of Christ by arguing that Jesus was an ESFJ. Such an argument reflects too small a view of His divine nature.

Effects of Radical Conversion

A second alternative explanation offered by leaders of the Boston Church of Christ is that the observed changes in psychological type scores may simply reflect the effects of radical conversion from non-Christian backgrounds. They pointed out that the majority of their members did not grow up in churches of Christ, but converted from non-Christian backgrounds. They correctly suggested that the comparative study I did among members of churches of Christ that are not identified with the discipling movement was not a fair comparison in this regard. It is likely that around 75 percent of those individuals grew up in churches of Christ. Leaders of the Boston Church of Christ argued that people who have experienced radical conversion from non-Christian backgrounds may tend to exaggerate the difference between what they were and what they are now.

I replied that such an explanation might account for the *degree* of change in psychological type scores, but that it would not explain the *pattern* of convergence in a single type. Furthermore, in such a case, the present distribution would have been closer to population norms than the past distribution. What was actually observed was that the past distribution was the closest to population norms while the present and future distributions increasingly deviated from those norms. However, since the original comparative study in other churches of Christ included many individuals whose experiences were not comparable to the experiences of most Christians in the Boston church, leaders of that church asked that additional studies be done.

One of these follow-up studies involved going back into other churches of Christ. This time, however, the only individuals included in the study were those who had recently experienced radical conversion from non-Christian backgrounds. Results of this study did not support the alternative explanation offered by leaders of the Boston church. The pattern in this study was not similar to the pattern observed in the Boston Church of

Christ the way they thought it would be. Instead, it was very similar to the original study in churches of Christ not affiliated with the discipling movement. There were no statistically significant changes in psychological type scores. The past, present, and future distributions did not differ significantly. There was no convergence in a single type.

Another follow-up study involved going back into the data from the Boston Church of Christ. This time, however, there was a comparison of those who had grown up in churches of Christ and those who experienced radical conversion from non-Christian backgrounds. Results of this study did not support the alternative explanation offered by leaders of the Boston church. The pattern among their members who had grown up in churches of Christ was not similar to the original study in churches of Christ not identified with the discipling movement the way they thought it would be. Instead, the pattern was very similar to that of those members in the Boston congregation who had experienced radical conversion from non-Christian backgrounds. There was a high degree of change in psychological type scores. There was the same pattern of significant differences among the past, present, and future distributions. There was also the same pattern of convergence in the same psychological type: ESFJ.

Individuals with a High Need for Control

There is a third alternative explanation of the observed pattern of changing psychological type scores in the Boston Church of Christ. This explanation was not offered by leaders of the Boston congregation. It was offered, instead, by people outside the discipling movement who are sympathetic toward that movement. Changes in psychological type scores, according to this explanation, may simply be the result of reaching individuals with a high need for control. This explanation in a different form was advanced by some defenders of the discipling movement before this study was conducted in the Boston Church of Christ.

According to this argument, the Boston Church of Christ and other discipling churches are justified in using high levels of control over their members—even if this control has some harmful side effects—because they are assumed to be attracting individuals with a psychological need for such control. It may be true that discipling churches are attracting individuals who come from non-Christian backgrounds and therefore may need closer supervision and more guidance than would be the case with someone who grew up in the church. That is not the same thing, however, as saying that their members have a psychological need for high levels of control.

With this argument in mind, I conducted a second psychological study in the Boston Church of Christ. This study involved the two newest converts from each of the 35 House Churches that were in operation at that time. These individuals were given a personality test called "FIRO-B."[2] The letters stand for Fundamental Interpersonal Relations Orientation in regard to Behavior. This instrument measures expressed and wanted levels of inclusion, control, and affection behavior. The focus of the study was on the "wanted control" scores of these newest converts in the Boston Church of Christ. Results of this study indicated that only a few had high wanted control scores. Most were in the moderate range. Some had low wanted control scores. The overall pattern was normal. Several had higher scores on wanted inclusion or wanted affection than on wanted control.

The results of this study did not support the view that the Boston Church of Christ is attracting people with a psychological need for high levels of control. They are reaching a wide range of people with normal and diverse psychological needs. The high level of control that they exercise over their members cannot be justified on the basis of any psychological need for such control. Indeed, that high level of control may be responsible, at least in part, for the observed pattern of changing psychological type scores.

Objections to Diversity

Results of the psychological type study among members of the Boston Church of Christ clearly indicate that something is causing their members to deny their true type and try to become copies of someone else. Results of the various follow-up studies show that the alternative explanations offered by leaders of the Boston Church of Christ and others should not be accepted. These changes cannot be explained by arguing that Jesus was an ESFJ. They cannot be explained as exaggerations caused by the effects of radical conversion from non-Christian backgrounds. They cannot be explained or justified as being a result of reaching people with a psychological need for high levels of control. There is something in the discipling methodology producing this unhealthy pattern. Whatever it is, it should be changed.

This leaves defenders of the discipling movement with only one argument. They cannot deny that the psychological type scores are changing and converging in a single type. They cannot deny that the members are being made over after the image of the group norm. They cannot deny that the discipling methodology is producing this effect. Their last line of defense, therefore, is to argue that this pattern is acceptable—that diversity in psychological type is not good and that Christians ought to change psychological type and become more and more similar to one another.

Psychological type theory teaches that one should avoid trying to change psychological type. What some people hear in that statement is simply that one should avoid change. They take such statements as an excuse for a refusal to change inappropriate behaviors or a refusal to grow up. Some people have misused psychological type theory in that way, but that is not what psychological type theory teaches.

Good personality growth is a goal that is shared by type theory and the world's great religions. Such growth, maturation, and development requires change. What type theory seeks to point out is that healthy growth takes place within a person's true type and does not require denying one's true type and trying to become a copy of someone else. What is involved here is a tension between the need to achieve one kind of change and the need to avoid another kind of change. Change is healthy when it is defined as growth, maturation, or development within a person's true type. Change is not healthy when it is defined as denying one's true type and trying to become another type. There is no conflict between Christianity and type theory. Every change that Christianity requires in human behavior can take place within a person's true type. No one needs to change psychological type in order to grow as a Christian.

. . . healthy growth takes place within a person's true type and does not require denying one's true type and trying to become a copy of someone else.

In the current debate over the methods and doctrines of the discipling movement, it is important to avoid two opposite but equally dangerous extremes. The psychological study conducted in the Boston Church of Christ illustrates one of these extremes. They are producing the wrong kind of change. They are producing conformity in psychological type. That is unnatural, unhealthy, and dangerous. But the Boston Church of Christ is not trying to produce changes in psychological type scores. They have no interest in psychological type theory. What they want is for their members to grow spiritually, to become more like Jesus Christ, and to be more evangelistic. They want to help their members overcome temptation and abstain from various sins. The way they go about doing this, however, is producing an unintended byproduct that is not healthy. They are changing personalities by making their members over after the group norm. That extreme must be avoided.

An opposite and equally dangerous extreme is to make no real effort at all to help Christians make the changes in their lives that they really ought to make. Some churches of Christ that are not affiliated with the discipling movement provide little if any individual assistance to Christians in an effort to help them grow as they should. Both of these extremes are wrong. Both should be avoided. The Holy Spirit changes people when they become Christians—but not by making us identical in psychological type. The growth that comes from the Holy Spirit produces a body with many different members that perform many different functions in many different ways. Influences that cause people to become identical in psychological type do not come from the Holy Spirit.

NOTES FOR CHAPTER 3

[1]W. Harold Grant, Magdala Thompson, and Thomas E. Clarke, *From Image to Likeness* (New York: Paulist Press, 1983).

[2]For the theory behind this test see: Will Shutz, *The Interpersonal Underworld* (Palo Alto, California: Consulting Psychologists Press, 1972). For details regarding administration and interpretation see: Will Shutz, *Manual for the FIRO Tests* (Palo Alto; California: Consulting Psychologists Press, 1972).

CHAPTER

4

A DISCUSSION OF DIFFERENCES

What is it about the Boston Church of Christ that causes the changes in psychological type scores discussed in the previous chapters? Since other churches of Christ are not producing this effect, the cause or causes must be found in the differences between the Boston Church of Christ and other churches of Christ.

When Christians who are not identified with the discipling movement attend the Sunday morning worship assembly of the Boston Church of Christ, they often report that they see nothing wrong. What they observe in the worship assembly is very similar to what they see in other churches of Christ. The doctrines that they hear preached in the sermons are the same as those preached in other churches of Christ. Visitors notice that the Boston Church of Christ has elders, deacons, and evangelists. The organization, therefore, seems to be the same as other churches of Christ. First impressions of the Boston congregation are typically very favorable.

Several obvious differences between the Boston Church of Christ and other churches of Christ have little to do with fundamental doctrinal issues. The congregation is made up primarily of college students and young adults. They meet in a rented sports arena. They have only one meeting a week when the entire congregation comes together. Each member of the Boston church is required to attend Sunday morning worship, Wednesday evening House Church, and at least one Bible Talk a week. There are over 60 House Church meetings throughout the Boston area each Wednesday evening. These are Bible classes designed to teach the members. There are over 260 Bible Talks in the Boston area each week. These are small group meetings designed to reach non-members. Each member is expected to invite at least 10 people a week to attend Bible Talk.

Most observers from other churches of Christ do not see these differences as being significant. Most recognize these as areas where local congregations are free to adapt to their own situations in their own ways. Some have questions about the way some of these things are done, but most do not raise any objections over these incidental differences.

There are, however, some differences between the Boston Church of Christ and other churches of Christ that are fundamental. Some of these differences involve factors that may be responsible for producing the unhealthy personality changes observed in the psychological type study of the Boston church. When I presented my report of that study to the leaders of the Boston church, I made several specific suggestions regarding changes that I felt were needed to correct that situation. It was my understanding that they agreed to make these changes. My plan at that time was to wait one year and then return to Boston to conduct a psychological type study among the new converts brought into the congregation after these changes had been made. I was confident that such a study would find that the problems had been corrected and that personalities were no longer being changed to conform to the group norm. In November of 1986, however, I learned that the changes were never made. I continue to receive reports from other churches of Christ in the area and from counselors who work with the emotional and spiritual problems of those who drop out of the Boston Church of Christ. These reports clearly indicate that the changes I suggested have not been implemented. Indeed, the congregation appears to be moving further and further away from what other churches of Christ would regard as true New Testament Christianity.

. . . the congregation appears to be moving further and further away from what other churches of Christ would regard as true New Testament Christianity.

Approach to Discipling

Other churches of Christ do not generally use the word "discipling" the way it is used in the Boston Church of Christ and other congregations that identify with the discipling movement. Other churches of Christ, however, are concerned about teaching their members and helping them grow spiritually. They just believe in calling Bible things by Bible names and they do not believe that the New Testament ever talks about discipling someone who is already a disciple. If they use the word "discipling" at all, they would generally use it to describe the process of disciple making. They would use other words to describe the process of disciple building. The fundamental differences in regard to discipling, however, go far beyond words.

What the Boston Church of Christ calls "discipling" involves a network of hierarchical relationships. In other churches of Christ, disciple-building relationships involve peers. When I presented the report of my psychological study, the leaders of the Boston congregation denied that they practiced hierarchical discipling. But when the members of that congregation turned in their psychological type forms, I had them write on those forms the name of the person most responsible for discipling them. I then charted the relationships and all the arrows pointed straight up their hierarchy. New converts are discipled by older converts. The older converts are discipled by Bible Talk leaders. The Bible Talk leaders are discipled by House Church leaders. The House Church leaders are discipled by zone evangelists. The zone evangelists are discipled by Kip McKean and the elders. It is only the preacher and two elders who list one another as disciplers in peer relationships. Furthermore, in my interviews with many of the members of the Boston church, I asked them to name the person who was discipling them and to name the people they were discipling. I never had the same people listed in answer to both questions except with the preacher and two elders. Since that time, articles in the bulletin of the Boston congregation have stated that in discipling there must be a clear understanding as to who is doing the discipling and who is being discipled.

When discipling resembles a multi-level marketing system, it is inevitable that people will be influenced to become like the group norm. To avoid the kind of personality manipulation observed in the psychological type study of the Boston Church of Christ, disciple-building relationships need to be peer relationships. Making such a change should not be too difficult for the discipling churches. They have placed great emphasis on the "one another" passages in the Bible. Reciprocal relationships between equals would be consistent with the "one another" passages. Hierarchical relationships are not.

Discipling, in the Boston model, involves each member having only one discipler. In other churches of Christ, disciple-building relationships involve several close personal friends. A new convert who identifies with several Christian friends is likely to filter out the many ways in which they are different and focus on what they have in common. The new convert, therefore, is much more likely to identify with the Christ in each of these friends and less likely to be made over after the image of just one friend.

From the time when the discipling movement first began among churches of Christ at the Crossroads congregation, discipling has focused on confession. New converts are taught that they must confess their sins to their disciplers. If they seem reluctant to do so, they are asked a lot of personal questions. If they still have no sins to confess, they are asked to read 1 John 1:8-10 and they are told that a refusal to admit sin is sin within itself. That at least gives them something to confess. I suggested to the leaders of the Boston Church of Christ that an emphasis on Bible study and prayer would be much better than this emphasis on confession. They said that they had already started moving in that direction. However, almost two years have passed since that meeting and the reports I am getting from the Boston area strongly indicate that the Boston Church of Christ still emphasizes confession as an essential part of discipling.

The Boston church uses James 5:16 to justify their requirement that Christians confess their sins to their disciplers. Other churches of Christ do not believe that this verse teaches any such thing. New Testament scholars are virtually unanimous in teaching that this verse simply means that if I sin against you, I must confess it to you and if you sin against me you must confess it to me. Every other passage of Scripture on the subject of confession teaches that sins must be confessed to God and to the individuals we have wronged. No other verse in the entire Bible says anything about confessing to a non-involved third party. The Boston Church of Christ rejects the Roman Catholic doctrine of auricular confession. They do not believe that sins must be confessed to a priest. What they are practicing, however, is seen by other churches of Christ as being a form of auricular confession.

Every other passage of Scripture on the subject of confession teaches that sins must be confessed to God and to the individuals we have wronged. No other verse in the entire Bible says anything about confessing to a non-involved third party.

Other churches of Christ recognize that self-disclosure can have therapeutic value in some cases for some people. There was a self-disclosure fad in pop psychology in the 1960s. There were all sorts of T-Groups, Encounter Groups, Sensitivity Training Groups, and the like. People were encouraged to bare their souls to these groups. The experience helped some people and hurt others. Psychologists later did some research on the effects of self-disclosure. They found that *when there is too much self-disclosure that comes too soon in a relationship or that comes under too much pressure, it creates a potentially manipulative, destructive, and dangerous relationship.* Christians need to have friends they can really trust. It often helps to confide in a friend. Self-disclosure, however, is not always helpful. Some personality types seem to benefit from self-disclosure much more than others. Many faithful Christians have grown to maturity in Christ without ever having much experience with self-disclosure.

Furthermore, self-disclosure is not what James 5:16 is talking about.

Other churches of Christ believe that the work of disciple building needs to be done with the recognition that some people benefit from self-disclosure much more than others. They contend that no one has the right to bind on all Christians a practice that may be helpful for only some. They claim that no one has the right to make self-disclosure a law when God has not made it a law. The rules of the Boston Church of Christ require that men disciple men and women disciple women. Other churches of Christ might see that as a good practice generally for disciple-building relationships, but they would not accept it as a rule that must always be followed.

Other churches of Christ believe that any self-disclosure that is done needs to be done in the right way. It takes time to build trust. It takes a lot of shared experience to build relationships to the point where self-disclosure is appropriate. The interviews I had with members of the Boston Church of Christ convinced me that they are getting into some really heavy self-disclosing long before they have had the time to build trusting relationships. When I asked members of the Boston congregation to identify the person most responsible for discipling them, at least one fourth could not correctly spell the name of that person. That does not sound like the kind of relationships where intensely personal self-disclosure would be appropriate.

Other churches of Christ believe that if self-disclosure is going to take place in disciple-building relationships, those involved must be taught to treat things disclosed as being strictly confidential. Such matters must not be revealed to others without the permission of the individual involved. All too often in the Boston system, however, things disclosed to a discipler one day are known all the way up the discipling hierarchy the next day. The discipling hierarchy thus becomes a glorified informant network. As such, it is an effective means of control—but it is not a good atmosphere for healthy disciple building.

In the Boston Church of Christ, those being discipled are taught that they must submit to their discipler. Passages such as Hebrews 13:17 have been taken out of context to justify this requirement of submission. In the past two years, I have interviewed many Christians in the Boston congregation and many others who were once involved in the discipling movement in Boston or elsewhere. Many of these individuals told me that their disciplers required total submission without question. A large majority of those individuals told me that their disciplers often gave orders that had nothing to do with spiritual matters. Those being discipled were told what courses to take in school, what field to major in, what career to enter, whom to date or not date, and even whom to marry or not marry. Leaders of the discipling movement admit that such abuses have taken place, but they claim that these are merely the excesses of young people with more zeal than judgment. The system, however, puts young people without much experience or judgment into positions where such abuses are likely to happen. Furthermore, many of these young people have now had plenty of time to grow up and yet they are still involved in the same abuses.

The Boston Church of Christ now teaches that Christians must obey their disciplers even in matters of opinion where there is no biblical justification for the orders given. They claim that Hebrews 13:17 refers to matters of opinion and they claim that it includes the authority of evangelists, elders, zone leaders, House Church leaders, Bible Talk leaders, and disciplers. The Boston church claims that they have corrected any possible abuses of authority by giving their members the right of appeal. If a member is given an order by a discipler that the member does not want to obey, that member has the right of appeal to the Bible Talk leader.

> The Boston Church of Christ now teaches that Christians must obey their disciplers even in matters of opinion where there is no biblical justification for the orders given.

The appeal can be taken all the way up the hierarchy to the House Church leader, zone evangelist, and even to the elders and the lead evangelist. But if the order given by the discipler is approved by these leaders, that member is required to obey. The only exceptions are that members are not expected to obey an order that would require them to go against the Bible or to violate their own conscience. The trouble, however, is that the leaders are the ones who decide what the Bible teaches and thus what a person's conscience should require.

Discipling churches teach that Christians are supposed to imitate their disciplers. They support this doctrine with verses where Paul told Christians to imitate him. One of these verses is 1 Corinthians 11:1 where Paul said, "Be imitators of me, as I am of Christ." Other churches of Christ believe that all Christians are supposed to imitate about Paul is his imitation of Jesus Christ. If Paul imitated Jesus and Timothy imitated Paul and someone else imitated Timothy—by the time the chain gets down to us there would be little real Christianity left.

When a church practices hierarchical discipling with each Christian having a single or primary discipler to whom sins must be confessed and who must be obeyed and imitated, it is inevitable that the church will make people over after the image of the group norm. That hurts people psychologically and spiritually.

Doctrine Follows Practice

Throughout its history, the church has been plagued by pragmatism. The pragmatist finds methods that seem to work and employs those methods. If challenged, the pragmatist will go to the Bible to find ways to justify the methods he has already decided to use. That approach is quite different from the approach taught in the Bible. Christians are supposed to begin by going to the Bible to find what God wants them to do. Doctrine must come first. Doctrine must be the foundation for practice. With the pragmatists, however, doctrine follows practice.

The practices associated with discipling that were discussed in the previous section do not grow out of a solid theological foundation. They were not discovered through careful Bible study. They grew out of a pragmatic concern for finding methods that seem to work. Doctrines are now being developed to justify the practices. Discipling, however, is not the only area where doctrine appears to follow practice. Most of the differences between the discipling churches and other churches of Christ are in the area of practices. Only in recent years have doctrinal differences emerged.

Organizational Differences

In the discipling movement among churches of Christ, preachers appear to have more decision-making and administrative authority than the elders have. In Boston, for example, decisions are made in meetings of the elders and evangelists. I attended all of those meetings for two weeks on my first visit to Boston. I have interviewed many others who have observed these meetings. One thing that all of us noticed is that Kip McKean presides at these meetings, makes virtually all of the decisions, and gives instructions to the other evangelists and to the elders. I asked the elders of the Boston Church of Christ about this practice—which is most unusual among churches of Christ. They defended the practice with the claim that they recognize talent and use it. Observers from other churches of

Christ have never questioned McKean's ability as an executive or administrator. What they have questioned is the propriety of any eldership turning over that much authority to any preacher.

The discipling movement, of course, did not begin among churches of Christ where local congregations are led by a plurality of men serving as elders, overseers, and shepherds with the assistance of deacons and ministers. It began in denominations where each local congregation is led by one pastor. What developed in that context was a discipling hierarchy with one pastor at the top of the pyramid. As the discipling movement spread into churches of Christ, many observers believe that the real power has been held by the preachers with elders serving only as figureheads and with deacons playing only a minor role. If discipling churches have elders, they typically have only two. Some observers believe that this is because two elders are enough to meet the requirement of plurality, but not enough to get in the way of the real power structure.

Many observers have noticed that when elders are selected in discipling churches, it is the preacher who selects them. In cases that I have observed personally, preachers for discipling churches have recruited qualified men to join their congregations and become "elder interns." If they successfully complete a period of discipling, the preacher appoints them as elders. Other churches of Christ follow the pattern of Acts 6:1-6 in the selection of elders or deacons. In this case, the congregation did the selecting of the seven special servants and the apostles appointed those men the congregation selected. Other churches of Christ believe that a man would be lording it over the church if he became an elder without the consent of the members. Leaders of the discipling movement claim that their congregations have so many new converts that their members would not know how to select qualified elders or deacons. In Acts 6, however, the Jerusalem congregation was made up of new converts and yet the apostles trusted them to select these leaders.

. . . when elders are selected in discipling churches, it is the preacher who selects them.

For several years, the practice of discipling churches has differed from that of other churches of Christ in regard to the authority of the preacher. Until recently, however, the discipling churches denied that their practice differed from that of other churches of Christ. They claimed that their congregations were led by their elders. They are no longer making that claim. They have started picking up the doctrine of evangelistic oversight that was advocated, examined, and rejected in the early days of the Restoration Movement.

According to the doctrine of evangelistic oversight, the evangelist is in charge of a congregation until elders are appointed. When elders are appointed, the evangelist does not just appoint those elders selected by the congregation—following the selection pattern of Acts 6. Instead, the evangelist selects the elders. In the Boston version of the old evangelistic oversight doctrine, the evangelist continues to make most of the decisions even after elders are appointed. Whether in doctrine or just in practice, the elders of the Boston Church of Christ function primarily in an advisory role. It is their lead evangelist who is at the top of their hierarchy. Now they have gone one step further by teaching that their lead evangelist is at the top of a hierarchy of congregations. They use Ephesians 4:16 to support their claim with the argument that the evangelists are the ligaments mentioned in the NIV translation of this verse—the ligaments that hold the various congregations together. They claim, therefore, that the evangelist is an officer of the universal church, not just a ministering servant in a local church. That would give their lead evangelist the right to direct congregations throughout the world.

Now they have gone one step further by teaching that their lead evangelist is at the top of a hierarchy of congregations.

The trouble with this interpretation is that this is not what the verse teaches. The ligaments of Ephesians 4:16 are the Christians, not just the evangelists. The body they hold together is primarily the local church, not the universal church. Other churches of Christ do not believe that the evangelist has or needs any authority other than the authority to preach the gospel. The practice of the discipling churches has been consistent for several years with the old rejected doctrine of evangelistic oversight. Now their doctrine is getting in line with their practice.

Critics of the discipling movement have objected to the practice of having pastoral functions performed by people who are not qualified to be elders. When there are only two elders in a large congregation and the pastoral functions are delegated from elders to zone evangelists to House Church leaders to Bible Talk leaders to disciplers, the average member has very little contact with the shepherds. The discipling hierarchy of the Boston church is an efficient means of control. Critics, however, deny that this hierarchy is a proper way for elders to perform their spiritual counseling-teaching duties as shepherds.

Leaders of the discipling movement defend hierarchical delegated shepherding with the example of Exodus 18:13-26 where Moses instituted a judicial system with four levels. Disputes went first to a ruler in charge of 10 people. If the dispute could not be settled at that level, it went to a ruler in charge of 50 people.

Disputes unresolved at that level went to a ruler in charge of 100 people. Appeals from that level went to a ruler in charge of 1,000 people. The only cases that were brought to Moses were those that could not be resolved in a lower court. This was an effective judicial system. Military organizations have found a similar chain of command to be an efficient means of control. But there is nothing in the Bible to indicate that God intended this Jewish judicial system to be a model for the shepherding work of elders in local congregations.

Critics argue that hierarchical delegated shepherding gives too many pastoral functions to young people at the bottom of the pyramid who are not qualified to be pastors. James S. Woodroof preaches for the Church of Christ in Burlington, Massachusetts. He said that in his congregation there are many people who by reason of years ought to be teachers and they are not—but in the nearby Boston Church of Christ there are many people who by reason of years ought not to be teachers and they are.

Critics argue that hierarchical delegated shepherding gives too many pastoral functions to young people at the bottom of the pyramid who are not qualified to be pastors.

Differences regarding Baptism

Discipling churches delay baptism until they are convinced that the person really believes and has fully repented and is totally committed. Other churches of Christ do not believe that Christians have the right to judge such matters. If people say that they believe, that they have repented, and that they want to be baptized, other churches of Christ baptize them. There are, of course, extreme cases that are exceptions to this rule. But if other churches of Christ are going to err in this matter, they want it to be in the direction of baptizing those who request baptism. Discipling churches seem to err in the direction of withholding baptism from those who are ready for baptism.

The elders of a discipling church in Florida refused permission for a man to be baptized because he had not quit a job that required him to work on Sundays. He was looking for another job, but did not feel it would be fair to his family for him to quit his present job until he found another. In the meantime, he knew that he needed to be baptized for the remission of his sins. Other churches of Christ would have baptized him.

Leaders of a discipling church in Denver, Colorado, met with the elders of the Bear Valley Church of Christ to discuss their differences. Leaders of this discipling church were asked if they would baptize a person who said he believed in Jesus Christ, had repented of his sins, and wanted to become a Christian—but that he did not want to attend Bible Talk meetings because he wanted to do his evangelism in a different way. They said that they would refuse to baptize such a person because he is not yet converted.

Many observers believe that discipling churches delay baptism until the disciplers are convinced that the prospective converts will submit to their authority without question. The issue is not their readiness to obey the gospel, but their willingness to submit to the control system provided in the discipling hierarchy.

Many observers believe that discipling churches delay baptism until the disciplers are convinced that the prospective converts will submit to their authority without question.

Many discipling churches have a tradition of requiring two confessions before baptism. First they ask, "Do you believe with all your heart that Jesus is the Christ, the Son of God?" After an affirmative answer, they ask this second question, "What is your good confession?" The answer is "Jesus is Lord!" Leaders of the discipling movement admit that this second confession is not required. They understand that the first confession implies the second. That understanding, however, has not filtered down through the discipling hierarchy. Some of the young people at the bottom of the pyramid believe that a baptism is not valid unless both confessions were verbalized.

Many people who have come to discipling churches from other churches of Christ have been taught by their disciplers that they must be rebaptized. Leaders of the Boston Church of Christ admit that around five percent of all their baptisms are such rebaptisms. Interviews with leaders of other churches of Christ in the Boston area indicate that over half of those who have gone to the Boston Church of Christ from these other congregations have been rebaptized. When the Crossroads Church of Christ sent campus ministers to work in

Interviews with leaders of other churches of Christ in the Boston area indicate that over half of those who have gone to the Boston Church of Christ from these other congregations have been rebaptized.

other churches of Christ, such rebaptism accounted for a lot more than five percent of their total baptisms. Now that the Boston church is taking over the Crossroads-type churches, many of their members are being rebaptized. The psychological function of the rebaptism phenomenon is similar to the psychological function of the "replanting" terminology used when the Boston church takes over a congregation: both serve to deny the validity of the previous religious experience of the individual. This cuts that individual off from his or her roots spiritually and thus gives the discipler more power to control and change that individual.

Judgmental Attitude

What is happening in the Boston Church of Christ is a good example of how the discipling churches view other churches of Christ. When half of the people who come to the Boston Church of Christ from other churches of Christ in the area are rebaptized, that gives these other congregations the impression that they are not regarded as being faithful Christians since their baptism is not considered valid. This impression is reinforced when new converts in the Boston church are told not to attend the other churches of Christ in the area. Leaders of the Boston church excuse this with the claim that relationships are important and these new converts would not have such relationships in these other congregations. It is true that relationships are important, but that does not justify telling new converts that other churches of Christ in the area are dead, that they are not spiritual, or that they could not provide the discipling that the new converts need. Interviews with over 100 new converts in the Boston church and over 100 others who have left the Boston church have convinced me that these judgmental comments about other churches of Christ are the rule, not the exception.

When discipling churches call themselves the "remnant," this gives the same impression. Leaders of the discipling movement try to explain that they are just talking about a small group of Christians whom God uses to achieve great growth, but they have tied their use of the "remnant" terminology to the Bible and in the Bible it was only the remnant that was faithful: all others were lost.

Discipling churches now constitute a totally separate fellowship. They cooperate with one another. They are in competition with churches of Christ that are not identified with the discipling movement. This competition clearly implies a judgment that these other churches of Christ are unfaithful. In recent years, leaders of the discipling movement have become increasingly open in expressing their judgment that the discipling churches are the only faithful churches and that all other churches of Christ are unfaithful.

In recent years, leaders of the discipling movement have become increasingly open in expressing their judgment that the discipling churches are the only faithful churches and that all other churches of Christ are unfaithful.

Gift Projection

Gift projection is the tendency of some Christians to judge other Christians by our gifts and to insist that all other Christians must develop our gifts and get involved in our ministries in order to be faithful. This attitude ignores what the Bible teaches about different Christians having different gifts and being involved in different ministries.

Other churches of Christ believe that all Christians should be involved in evangelism in some way, but they do not insist that all be involved in the same way. They believe that all Christians should share their faith, but they do not require that all Christians do this in the same way.

My study of the Boston Church of Christ convinced me that only 10 to 15 percent of their members had ever converted anyone. What I am talking about are those who have taken a leading role in the teaching and persuading that brought others to the point of obedience. I told the leaders of that congregation that they ought to rejoice that so many of their members were involved in evangelism at this level. But I also told them that they ought to rejoice in the fact that virtually all the rest of their members are involved in evangelism in other ways. I call them the "grinners," although that is not a title the Boston church recognizes. The grinners are the people who invite at least 10 others to Bible Talk each week. They regularly attend Bible Talk. They do not lead the Bible Talk. They just sit there and grin and say "Amen." When the people they bring with them to Bible Talk get interested enough to be receptive to the gospel, it is usually the Bible Talk leader who does what they call the one-on-one teaching. But the teaching is not really one-on-one. It is two-on-one, because the grinner is right there supporting the process, grinning, and occasionally saying, "You need to do what he says." After this person is baptized, the grinner becomes his discipling partner. It seems to me that the grinners are being evangelistic. They are sharing their faith. But most of the leaders I talked to in the Boston church felt that the grinners needed to repent and get with the program.

Discipling churches talk a lot about being "fruitful" or "productive." Some have taught that the only fruit of a Christian is another Christian. That is not the way the Bible uses the fruit metaphor. Leaders of the Boston Church of Christ understand that, but members of the congregation still think that making converts is the only way to be fruitful or productive.

The Boston congregation provides only one role model for their members. The people they brag on are those who are making a lot of converts. I urged the leaders of that congregation to start providing other role models. I suggested that they brag on some of their grinners who never have converted anyone, but who are at least involved in the evangelistic effort and who help the church in other ways. The elders sent me a tape of one sermon where Kip McKean did this, but it will take a lot more than one sermon to overcome the influence of previous years.

Having just one role model may explain a part of the psychological manipulation discussed earlier. A church with only one role model is likely to make its members over after the image of that one model. This is especially likely to happen in a church where the members soon realize that there is only one way to advance in leadership. In discipling churches, the way members prove that they are qualified for various leadership roles is by making a lot of converts and helping those converts make a lot of converts. What this system ignores is the importance of many other gifts that are needed in a congregation.

Critics of the discipling movement believe that these churches have never really understood the theology of gifts, the value of diversity, or the concept of the church as a body with many different members that perform many different functions in many different ways. Several critics have suggested that discipling churches resemble a giant reproductive system rather than a whole body.

Legalism

The public teaching of discipling churches proclaims the doctrine of salvation by grace. That, however, is not what filters down through the discipling hierarchy. What people at the bottom of the pyramid hear is that they must earn their way to heaven by the merit of their works.

Discipling churches have many arbitrary rules that have no biblical foundation. Some of these rules probably started as wise advice. However, what started as wise advice needed by some people in one place soon became fixed rules bound on everyone in many other congregations. Requiring that everyone have an hour a day of quiet time may be good advice, but God did not give this as a law. Those who have recently converted from non-Christian backgrounds might need some advice about whom to date or not date, but there is no law in the Bible requiring permission of a discipler before dating. Furthermore, the emphasis on rule keeping that spreads throughout the discipling process communicates the wrong message. Some Christians may be helped by suggested goals or targets in regard to their evangelism or other areas of Christian service, but those goals are not laws from God. An over-emphasis on goals and targets for evangelism communicates a message of justification by the merit of works.

Discipling churches have a practice of requiring prospective converts to write out a list of all the sins they have ever committed. Other churches of Christ find such a rule to be arbitrary at best. Many object to the practice even if it is not treated as a law. They feel that it suggests the wrong emphasis. This requirement about listing all sins prior to baptism suggests a works-centered gospel of the changed life. That is not the same thing as the gospel that changes lives—the Christ-centered gospel of grace.

There are significant differences between what the discipling churches teach publicly and what they communicate privately to their members.

There are significant differences between what the discipling churches teach publicly and what they communicate privately to their members. There are significant differences between what the discipling churches communicate verbally and what they communicate nonverbally. You cannot get a book that teaches you the Boston system. You have to go to Boston and be trained for at least a year. The reason for this is that the real message in the Boston Church of Christ is not the public message that is verbalized; it is the non-verbal message communicated privately by the nature and emphasis of the discipling hierarchy.

CHAPTER

5

DEALING WITH THE DISCIPLING DILEMMA

If members of the churches of Christ had only two alternatives—a discipling church or a non-evangelistic church—many would regard the discipling church as the lesser of the two evils. Churches of Christ that oppose the discipling movement need to face the most powerful and persuasive argument in favor of that movement and they need to face it head on. That argument is the pragmatic argument based on a comparison of results. Discipling churches are growing faster than other churches of Christ. They claim that this proves that they are right.

The gap between the growth of the discipling churches and other churches of Christ is significant, but it is not as great as the discipling churches have claimed. Other discipling churches are not generally growing as fast as the Boston Church of Christ. They are not generally growing as fast today as they were a few years ago. Furthermore, figures published by the Boston Church of Christ indicate that their net growth rate is not as high as they have claimed. If you count all those they have baptized and subtract those they have sent to mission fields, the result indicates a retention rate of only 65 percent, not the 75 percent they now claim or the 95 percent they used to claim. Some of these, of course, have moved away from the Boston area. The

Boston congregation, however, has not yet demonstrated a good retention rate among those who are converted in Boston and then move away. Their net growth rate, therefore, is not as high as they have claimed, but it is still higher than the growth rate of other churches of Christ.

It is important to notice, however, that other churches of Christ are not declining rapidly the way the discipling churches claim. It has been a cause of some concern to me that my own research has been used by the discipling churches to support their claim that other churches of Christ are declining rapidly. I have been doing survey research on patterns of growth and decline among churches of Christ in the United States for almost 20 years. These surveys probably provide the best available estimates of growth rates among churches of Christ in this nation. These surveys indicate that the rate of growth declined from 1965 (the date of the earliest survey) to 1980. But that was not a decline in total membership. Churches of Christ grew in this period. It was just the rate of growth that declined. The surveys indicate that in 1965 the rate of growth may have been as high as five percent per year. There was an average decline of one third of one percent per year from 1965 through 1980. If these survey estimates are accurate, growth stopped in 1980. Between 1980 and 1984, there appears to have been a decline of around 2.5 percent. In 1984, however, the pattern started to change. In 1985, there was a very small growth of 0.02 percent. In 1986, there was a more substantial growth of around 0.5 percent. These improvements do not reflect growth in the discipling churches. They have been studied separately. Churches of Christ that are not identified with the discipling movement have started growing again. The gap between the growth in the discipling churches and the growth in other churches of

Christ, therefore, is not as great as the discipling churches have claimed. That gap, however, is real. Discipling churches are growing faster than other churches of Christ and that fact is the most convincing argument in favor of the discipling movement.

The Problem with Pragmatism

The problem with the pragmatic argument based on a comparison of growth rates is that it proves too much. The discipling churches do not really believe that numerical growth is always proof of divine approval. Paul Yonggi Cho's Full Gospel Central Church in Seoul, Korea, has over half a million members. That makes that congregation the largest congregation in Christendom. Leaders of the discipling movement among churches of Christ do not regard the growth of Cho's congregation as proof of divine approval. The Jotabeche Methodist Pentecostal Church in Santiago, Chile, and the Congregacao Christa in Sao Paulo, Brazil, have experienced amazing growth—but leaders of the discipling movement among churches of Christ do not regard that growth as evidence of God's approval.

In the biblical record, some of God's greatest servants had little to show in the way of visible results. Noah was a preacher of righteousness who preached for 100 years while building the ark, but he converted only his wife, their three sons, and their wives. Jeremiah was a faithful prophet of God, but he was ignored and persecuted by the people of his generation. Success from God's perspective cannot always be measured in terms of immediate numerical church growth.

Christians should not be overly impressed by the pragmatic argument based on a comparison of growth rates. Church leaders, however, need to recognize that this pragmatic argument is very persuasive to many people. They need to be prepared, therefore, to explain why the discipling churches have grown faster than other churches of Christ.

Comparing Results

A part of the reason discipling churches are growing faster than other churches of Christ is that the discipling methods they use get a large number of members actively involved in evangelism as teachers. Churches that are not willing to practice gift projection or employ high pressure methods are not as likely to get that many members involved in this role. It remains to be seen, however, whether this approach can be sustained over a long period of time. Denominations where the discipling movement started did not find that this approach worked for more than about one generation. There are such tremendous time pressures in this approach that it tends to result in a major burn-out problem. The discipling movement has no real ministry to the weak. People either become super Christians at once or they drop out. In the denominations where the discipling movement started, internal problems killed or seriously limited the movement within little more than one generation.

Denominations where the discipling movement started did not find that this approach worked for more than about one generation.

Characteristics that are unique to the discipling movement do not account for most of the growth experienced by discipling churches. Among churches of Christ, discipling churches are not growing primarily because of what they are doing that other churches of Christ regard as being wrong. They are growing primarily because of what they are doing that is right.

One of the major reasons for the rapid growth of the Boston Church of Christ and its daughter churches is that planting new congregations is the most effective of all church growth strategies. Only five percent of all congregations grow after they are 25 years old. In the decade of the 1970s, every denomination in the United States that increased the number of local congregations grew in total membership and every denomination that reduced the number of local congregations declined in total membership. In virtually all of these cases, the increase in the number of congregations came before the increase in total membership. In the period between 1945 and 1965, churches of Christ were generally regarded as being one of the fastest-growing religious groups in the nation. It was in that period that churches of Christ started more new congregations than ever before. Few new congregations have been planted since 1965 and the rate of growth has declined since 1965.

Most churches of Christ that are not identified with the discipling movement are more than 25 years old. That is one of the reasons that they are not growing today as fast as the discipling churches. Within a generation, of course, many of the discipling churches will be more than 25 years old. The rate of growth has already begun to decline in the discipling churches that grew directly out of the work at Crossroads. The rate of growth has even started to decline in the Boston Church of Christ.

Another important reason for the rapid growth of the discipling churches such as the Boston Church of Christ is the staff-to-member ratio. At the time of my first visit in April of 1985, the Boston congregation had one full-time worker for every 28 members. Many of these were not considered "staff" by the Boston church. Most were full-time interns preparing for leadership of a church-planting team. But the way these interns were being trained involved spending less than half their time studying in the Boston School of World Missions and the rest of their time they learned by working the system. They were available for service as disciplers, Bible Talk leaders, House Church leaders, and whatever else might be needed. Gene Vinzant's survey of discipling churches in 1987, as reported in the last section of this book, found an average staff-to-member ratio of one to 40. The team that went into Toronto had only two who were called "evangelists," but they had more than two dozen others who spent full time in evangelistic work. They baptized 100 people in the first year, but if you took 25 or 30 young, energetic, zealous, dedicated, talented Christians and had them work full time in any major city, they would produce comparable results.

Churches of Christ that are not affiliated with the discipling movement typically have staff-to-member ratios of around one to 100. In the 1986 church growth survey, I asked how many of the baptisms came from the work of full-time ministers and how many came from the work of volunteer workers in the congregation. Results indicate that well over half of all the adult conversions in 1986 came from the work of full-time ministers.

There is still another factor to consider in explaining why the discipling churches are growing faster than other churches of Christ. This especially applies to the Boston congregation. Writers in the church growth field have suggested for many years that Christians need to experience the church at three levels: the assembly level, an intermediate group level about the size of a House Church in Boston or an adult Bible class in another congregation, and the small group level about the size of a Bible Talk group in Boston or a friendship circle in another congregation. Church growth researchers have found that it works best to bring new members in at the bottom rather than at the top. New members can be assimilated much better if their conversion and most of their teaching takes place at the small group level. It is easy then to get them into the intermediate and assembly levels.

New members can be assimilated much better if their conversion and most of their teaching takes place at the small group level.

This is the way the Boston Church of Christ assimilates their new members. Conversion takes place in the context of a Bible Talk group consisting generally of no more than 15 people. They may not even know about the Sunday morning assembly at the Boston Gardens until they are well into the teaching process. When they go to the Boston Gardens for their first experience with that large crowd, the people who are sitting around them are their friends from their Bible Talk group. Around that group are other people whom they have met at the Wednesday evening House Church meeting in their neighborhood. They do not feel that they are lost in a big crowd.

Churches of Christ that are not a part of the discipling movement typically bring people in at the top and try to push them down to the two lower levels. They may try to convert people at the assembly level. If they convert them in a one-on-one study, they bring them to the assembly. At the assembly they learn that they are supposed to attend Bible classes. Some of them never make it that far. Those who start attending Bible classes may learn about some small group meetings. Most never make it that far. The few who take part in small group meetings may learn that they are supposed to get involved in evangelism. Very few make it that far. It is quite possible, however, for congregations to get their members involved at all three levels and bring new members in at the small group level without ever becoming a part of the discipling movement.

One of the most impressive things about the Boston Church of Christ is what they are doing with their Bible Talk groups. Writers in the church growth field have suggested for many years that conversion requires a point of contact and a pathway. The point of contact is a way of meeting non-members. The pathway is the orderly sequence of events that can be expected to bring some of these non-members to the point of conversion. Churches of Christ that are not identified with the discipling movement used evangelistic meetings and evangelistic preaching in other church services as the point of contact a few generations ago. That worked with some people in previous generations. It does not work with most people today. These congregations did a lot of personal evangelism in small groups—a family or two of members studying with a family of non-members. These "cottage meetings," as they were called, proved to be effective in teaching many people. Sometimes people taught in this way had to be motivated from the pulpit before they made the decision to obey the gospel. The home Bible studies and evangelistic preaching brought many people to Christ a few years ago. In recent years, however, these methods have been less effective.

The secret of the Bible Talk approach is that it is a non-threatening way for a non-member to be introduced to the study of the Bible. Bible Talk lessons are simple, practical, applied studies that do not focus on controversial doctrinal issues. They provide an opportunity to get people into the Scriptures and to show them that the Bible is relevant to their lives and that Christ has answers to their problems. These occasions also provide an opportunity for several Christians to build relationships with the non-member visitors. Once the non-members get interested, they are receptive to the evangelistic study that follows.

> The secret of the Bible Talk approach is that it is a non-threatening way for a non-member to be introduced to the study of the Bible.

The psychological type theory that was discussed in Chapter 2 helps to explain why the Bible Talk approach is so effective. Psychological type preferences are related to learning styles. Extraverts learn best through participation in a group discussion. Introverts learn best through lecture, reading, or one-on-one conversation. The Bible Talk approach is ideal for extraverts. The evangelistic methods other churches of Christ use are ideal for introverts. Extraverts make up 70 percent of the population and introverts make up only 30 percent.

Sensors learn best when the study begins with practical applications, hands-on experience, and step-by-step instruction. That is the way Bible Talk lessons are conducted. Intuitors learn best when the study begins with the background theory, the big picture, meanings, and implications. Evangelism in other churches of Christ typically begins with theology. The effort is to change beliefs first and get people thinking right at the beginning. Then later—perhaps much later—the study can get around to practical applications. This approach is ideal for intuitors. Sensors make up 70 percent of the population and intuitors make up only 30 percent. Those who prefer both extraversion and sensing make up 49 percent of the population. The Bible Talk approach is ideal for them. Those who prefer both introversion and intuition make up nine percent of the population. The kind of evangelism other churches of Christ typically practice is ideal for them.

Considering this factor alone, discipling churches ought to be baptizing five times as many people as other churches of Christ. It would be possible, however, for other churches of Christ to use a similar small group approach to Bible study at this non-threatening, non-doctrinal level as a step toward more intense evangelism. They could do this without ever accepting any of the objectional features of the discipling movement.

Another significant reason for the rapid growth of the Boston Church of Christ is its emphasis on mission work. They believe that if they take the best people they have and send them to the mission field, the rest will get better. Each team they send out takes a tremendous amount of talent away from that church. But each time they send out a team, others rise up to take their place. Churches of Christ that are not affiliated with the discipling movement have fewer missionaries on the field today than they did 10 years ago. Many young people who want to do mission work have been frustrated by the refusal of congregations to support them or even consider their plea for help. Some of these very talented and dedicated young people have been attracted to the Boston Church of Christ because of its mission emphasis. That emphasis has helped the Boston church grow. The lack of mission emphasis has retarded the growth of other churches of Christ.

The lack of mission emphasis has retarded the growth of other churches of Christ.

Discipling churches place a major emphasis on interpersonal relationships. As this study has already made clear, I do not believe that they are doing it in the right way. They are, however, to be commended for at least trying to get people into relationships that help them grow spiritually. When I was growing up, we did not have "discipling partners," but we had friends. A few years ago, members of the churches of Christ in this nation did not go home from church alone. We either had someone over for Sunday dinner or we went home with someone else. And it was not just Sunday dinner.

Our social life throughout the week was centered around our association with other Christians. Furthermore, the relationship was not totally secular. We almost always got the song books out and sang together. We prayed together. We had some heated arguments about religion that at least had the merit of being Christ-centered, Bible-based discussions. We talked a lot about spiritual matters. We were into one another's lives spiritually. If people got out of line, we tried to correct them. It was spontaneous and unorganized, but I believe that we practiced the "one another" passages in the Bible.

Things have changed. Recently I have been doing some research on friendship patterns in churches of Christ. In this study I use a questionnaire that asks several things about friendships. All of this research has been done in churches that do not identify with the discipling movement. What I have found is that from 10 to 20 percent of the members of these congregations do not have any close personal friends at all in the congregation where they are members. From 20 to 30 percent of the members have not actually visited with a close personal friend in the congregation in the past year—counting visits in either person's home, going out to do something together, or just talking to one another regularly on the telephone. In the modern church, people come together as strangers and leave as strangers and their lives never touch.

In the modern church, people come together as strangers and leave as strangers and their lives never touch.

Another item on this questionnaire asks those who have friends in the church what they do when they get together with their friends away from the church building and organized church activities. At least 80 percent report having only a secular relationship. The

20 percent who pray together, study the Bible together, or engage in any other religious activity during friendship time report doing this only once a month on the average.

Discipling churches, in my opinion, are wrong in the way they are trying to structure interpersonal relationships—but they are right in their emphasis on how important these relationships are for spiritual growth. However, other churches of Christ could encourage healthy, supportive, nurturing, non-manipulative relationships without any of the errors associated with the disciplining movement.

Many church growth researchers and writers have noted that in recent years conservative denominations have generally grown while liberal denominations have generally declined. Other writers more recently have suggested that the real difference here is between distinctive churches and non-distinctive churches. Most conservative denominations are also very distinctive. Everyone knows who they are and what they stand for. Most liberal denominations are more ecumenical. They try to be all things to all men and it is harder to get a clear picture of just who they are and what they believe.

Among churches of Christ, those that appear to be growing the fastest are those that are clearly distinctive from the world and from other religious groups. Those that have become much less distinctive in recent years have stopped growing and are declining gradually. Those that are distinctive only in terms of internal brotherhood issues are declining rapidly. The Boston Church of Christ and other discipling churches are clearly in the category of those who are distinctive from the world and from other religious groups.

These are just a few of the reasons that help to explain why the discipling churches have been growing faster than other churches of Christ. One important reason that I should not overlook is the quality of the young people who have been attracted to this movement. The Boston Church of Christ has been especially successful in attracting some super people. Some of the most talented, dedicated, zealous Christians I have ever seen are in the Boston Church of Christ. I believe that those same people could have produced similar results without any of the objectionable features of the discipling movement.

One other factor must be mentioned, although it may be unique to Boston. The Boston Church of Christ has over 60 House Churches. These are organized to serve relatively small neighborhoods. Boston is somewhat different from many other major metropolitan areas in that its neighborhoods have a clear ethnic identity. As a result, the House Churches in Boston are relatively homogeneous. One is primarily Black. Another is primarily Hispanic. Another is Chinese. In one House Church, many of the people are of Italian ancestry. The Bible Talk groups serve even smaller geographic areas and thus are even more homogeneous.

There are limits to how heterogeneous an assembly-oriented church can become. The Boston Church of Christ has managed to become an extremely heterogeneous church at the assembly level because of its emphasis on two smaller levels of interaction. That same approach, however, would be possible in other churches of Christ without any of the abuses associated with the discipling movement.

Which Way the Church?

The title of this section is taken from Bob Hendren's excellent study of legalism in the discipling movement.[1] In that book, the author expresses his concern over the direction being taken by discipling churches. I share that concern, but I am also concerned about directions being taken by churches of Christ that oppose the discipling movement.

Leaders of the discipling movement among churches of Christ believe that their movement is the wave of the future. They believe that by the early part of the next century, they will have thousands of congregations and millions of members throughout the world. They also believe that churches of Christ that do not identify with the discipling movement will cease to exist within another generation or two. I do not share that view.

I believe that in its emphasis on control, the discipling movement has the seeds of its own destruction. Control is manipulative. Control is dehumanizing. Control is a sick way of relating. Some people say that a benevolent dictatorship is the most efficient form of government. If that is true, it is true for only a short period of time. People will not long endure such a system.

Leadership of the discipling movement has already shifted from Crossroads to Boston, but it is not likely to remain in Boston for more than a few years. As Boston moves in one direction, other centers of influence are likely to emerge and move in other directions. The discipling movement among churches of Christ, in my opinion, is likely to fragment before the end of this century. Some people who were attracted to this movement a few years ago have already been disillusioned and have left the movement. There will likely be many more defections from their ranks in the near future.

The wave of the future, however, is not likely to be found in those churches of Christ that over-react and go to an opposite extreme. Some congregations, in their effort to escape from Crossroads or Boston, are running all the way past Jerusalem and ending up in Babylon. The elders of one congregation recently told their members, "We forbid any evangelism except the preaching done at this building where we can make sure that it is doctrinally correct." They went on to condemn any kind of home Bible study or personal evangelism as being "the Crossword philosophy." That shows how little they know about what is going on.

Some congregations, in their effort to escape from Crossroads or Boston, are running all the way past Jerusalem and ending up in Babylon.

Some people in churches of Christ do not really know what the discipling movement is all about. They have heard about "Crossroadsism" and they know that they are against it. Since they do not know what "Crossroadsism" is, they apply that label to anything they do not like. Some have become almost paranoid in their negative over-reactions.

Elders of churches of Christ that are not identified with the discipling movement need to know what to do when they learn that their city has been targeted and that a discipling church is about to be planted in their area. The following advice is offered for whatever it may be worth to such elders.

Do not think that you can persuade the leaders of the discipling movement to stay away just because you ask them to stay away. They honestly believe that your congregation is unfaithful, spiritually dead, and lost. They believe that they will be doing your members a favor if they persuade them to leave your congregation and join their congregation.

Be informed. Do not believe everything you read about the discipling movement. Investigate for yourself. Learn the facts.

I believe that you should establish leader-to-leader communication, but I do not believe that it would be wise to provide a platform for the leaders of the discipling movement to use in teaching their false doctrines, recruiting your members, and sowing discord among brethren. I do not believe that it would be wise to open your pulpit to them or to have them speak at brotherhood-wide lectureships or workshops.

If your congregation is not active in local evangelism and mission work throughout the world, you need to recognize that your congregaton is ripe for a hostile takeover. Your members need to know that they can be involved in local evangelism and mission work without joining a discipling congregation. Remember also that it is not easy to steal sheep who are well fed.

If your congregation is not active in local evangelism and mission work throughout the world, you need to recognize that your congregation is ripe for a hostile takeover.

You need to be ready to reach and restore the many drop-outs who will be harmed psychologically and spiritually by their participation in this movement. The time when these problems are most likely to develop is when the young people in this movement reach mid-life. Falsification of psychological type produces a serious mid-life crisis. There will be major burn-out problems, serious depression, and a variety of other psychological and spiritual problems to resolve.

You should not, in my opinion, make it any more difficult than necessary for those who have been caught up in this movement to return to the fellowship of churches of Christ that do not identify with the discipling movement.

In rejecting the errors of the discipling movement, be careful not to throw out the baby with the bath water. You should test all things and hold fast to what is good (1 Thess. 5:21). Discipling churches are doing many things that are good. Do not reject the good when you reject what is bad. Allow room for diversity in the body of Christ. There are things that might not fit your congregation that might be both useful and proper in a different congregation.

Discipling churches are doing many things that are good. Do not reject the good when you reject what is bad.

Allow room for diversity in the body of Christ. There are things that might not fit your congregation that might be both useful and proper in a different congregation.

Help your members get into non-manipulative, nurturing, disciple-building relationships. I have found the study of psychological type theory to be useful in this regard. Things that help an extravert grow spiritually might not be helpful for an introvert. What is useful for a sensing type might be harmful for an intuitive type. Thinking types and feeling types need to be guided in different ways. Judging types and perceiving types follow different pathways to maturity in Christ. I believe that this, in part, is what Solomon was talking about in Proverbs 22:6 when he said, "Train up a child in his own way and even when he is old he will not depart from it." However, Carl Jung's theory of psychological types is only one of many systems for classifying individual differences. Much more needs to be learned and taught concerning the most effective disciple-building approaches for different kinds of people. Several writers from various religious groups have already started this effort.[2] Much more work is needed to apply these principles to the task of disciple-making and disciple-building among the heirs of the Restoration Movement.

In this concluding section, I have taken the liberty of offering some advice along with some speculations about what may happen in the future. You know, of course, that I am not a prophet. I do not know what the future holds. I do know Who holds the future and that is enough.

NOTES FOR CHAPTER 5

[1]Bob Hendren, *Which Way the Church* (Nashville, Tennessee: 20th Century Christian, 1985).

[2]There are several sources—in addition to those already mentioned—that are useful in this study. The following would provide a good introduction to the field.

Christopher Bryant, *Jung and the Christian Way* (Minneapolis, Minnesota: The Seabury Press, 1983).

Christopher Bryant, *Prayer and Different Types of People* (Gainesville, Florida: Center for Applications of Psychological Type, Inc., 1983).

Gary L. Harbaugh, *The Faith-Hardy Christian* (Minneapolis, Minnesota: Augsburg Publishing House, 1986).

Chester P. Michael and Marie C. Norrisey, *Prayer and Temperament* (Charlottesville, Virginia: The Open Door, Inc., 1984). Note: To understand this book by Michael and Norrisey, one should begin with a study of temperament theory in David Keirsey and Marilyn Bates, *Please Understand Me* (Del Mar, California: Prometheus Nemesis Books, 1978).

PART II

THE IMPACT OF THE DISCIPLING MOVEMENT ON MISSION WORK DONE BY THE CHURCHES OF CHRIST

by Howard W. Norton

ABOUT THE AUTHOR

Howard W. Norton is the chairman of the division of Bible at Oklahoma Christian College and editor of the *Christian Chronicle,* an international newspaper of the churches of Christ. He worked from 1961 to 1977 as a missionary in Sao Paulo, Brazil.

Norton was the associate editor of the Bible correspondence course entitled *What the Bible Says,* which circulates today in several different languages. He co-edited the book entitled *Steps into the Mission Field: Group Evangelism, from First Concepts to First Converts* (1978), which was written by the Sao Paulo Mission Team. He wrote *The Eldership and the Missionary: A Manual for Independent Missions,* the second edition of which was published in 1980.

He is one of three directors of the Pan American Lectureship. He takes a campaign group to Brazil and conducted meetings there each summer. Recently he served as the pulpit minister of the College Church of Christ in Oklahoma City.

Norton graduated from Abilene Christian University with his Bachelor of Arts degree in 1957, from the University of Houston with the Master of Arts degree in 1964, and from the Universidade de Sao Paulo with the Doctor of Human Sciences degree in 1981.

CHAPTER 6

MISSION WORK: IN SEARCH OF THE PERFECT SOLUTION

Mission work in churches of Christ has passed through at least four phases during the twentieth century. In each phase, churches of Christ have searched for the perfect solution for evangelizing the world.

Phase 1: Pre-World War II

First, there was the pre-World War II mission work that focused its attention on nations of the Far East and Africa. During that period evangelistic men and women searched for the solution to the problem of apathy toward world evangelism within the church. Names such as these deserve our grateful praise for their pioneering efforts to spread the word of God in the Orient and for their desire to stir interest at home: the J. M. McCalebs, Clara Elliott Bishop, Sarah Shepherd Andrews, the Barney D. Moreheads, the Orville Bixlers, Hettie Lee Ewing, the families of Harry R. and Herman J. Fox, and the George S. Bensons.

As pioneer missionary families worked to evangelize the Far East, other courageous families braved the mysteries of Africa in order to preach the gospel there. We remember people like the John Sherriffs, the W. N. Shorts, the Ray Lawyers, the John Dow Merritts, and the George M. Scotts, whose names became synonymous with African evangelism.

Their great spirit can be seen in a statement by George S. Benson: "I had rather be here in China teaching these poor people the way of life and enduring hardships for Jesus than to be anywhere else in the world."[1]

God, no doubt, knows other people whom we have not mentioned here but who lived and worked at great sacrifice in order to obey the Great Commission and seek the lost in strange and distant cultures. Whatever has been accomplished since those pre-World War II days is due in large part to the inspiration given to churches of Christ by those heroes of the faith whose task was difficult in a world where travel and communication were quite primitive compared to what we enjoy today.

Besides the isolation and loneliness felt by those brothers and sisters, who were separated by thousands of miles from families and friends, their greatest frustration probably centered in the lack of widespread interest among Christians in the United States for what they were trying to accomplish. A lack of financial and moral support here at home, coupled with a general lack of concern for evangelizing the world, stood in the way of fulfilling Christ's command to go and preach to the nations. They searched for a solution to these problems.

A lack of financial and moral support here at home, coupled with a general lack of concern for evangelizing the world, stood in the way of fulfilling Christ's command to go and preach to the nations.

Phase II: Post World War II

World War II was a turning point in the history of Christian mission work in churches of Christ. It appeared that this hated war would provide the very solution to the lack of missionary concern and become the means for stirring interest in world missions. In many ways, it did just that. Because of the war effort and the accompanying orders to travel as soldiers and sailors of the Allied Forces, young Americans from churches of Christ discovered parts of the world they never knew existed. Christian boys and men from Texas, Arkansas, Oklahoma, Tennessee, California, Alabama, and other stateside regions found themselves in foreign lands full of cities and towns with strange sounding names. To their astonishment, they could not find a single congregation of the churches of Christ in most of the places they visited.

Amazed that the gospel as they knew it had never reached those parts of the world, they vowed that when the bloody battles of World War II were over, they would see to it that the "enemy" they had seen during the fight for world peace would have the opportunity to hear and obey the good news about Jesus Christ. They promised themselves that they would do everything in their power to establish local congregations of the New Testament church among the people whose lostness had stirred such deep compassion in their hearts. For some of these soldiers, it meant that they would return to those foreign countries as evangelists with hearts on fire. Others would be responsible for supporting those who went to preach.

Meanwhile, Olan Hicks began the *Christian Chronicle,* a mission-minded newspaper, in 1943. In spite of a world with its attention focused on some of the greatest battles in the history of the world, Olan Hicks turned his attention to the unbelievable opportunities for evangelism and church growth that his visionary instincts predicted for churches of Christ in America, once World War II was over. He began to raise the consciousness of local churches in the United States, urging them to prepare to send missionaries all over the world just as soon as the war-torn nations opened their doors for the victorious Allies to come in and help them. Hicks and others like him realized that if the churches had performed their evangelistic task throughout the world in a more committed way prior to World War II, the destruction that swept large portions of the earth might never have happened.

Otis Gatewood was the first foreign evangelist of any religious group to enter Germany after World War II ended in Europe. One of the great Christian motivators of this century, his inspirational example and emotional appeals to the brotherhood for additional manpower sparked a missionary movement whose effects are still being felt today.

Unfortunately, many who responded to the call and went abroad to preach the gospel were unprepared for what they encountered. Individuals and married couples would often go alone to some mission point or else join a group of workers whom they had not really known prior to their arrival on the field. Those who did the latter were emotionally alone. Short tenures, broken spirits, dashed dreams, and even broken lives and families sometimes resulted from the sincere but frustrating experiences of those who had hoped to evangelize the world. The most common explanation for missionary failure was "loneliness," and the generally accepted perfect solution for this major occupational problem of foreign missions was "team evangelism." With the problem of apathy solved by World War II, it appeared that "team evangelism" was all that was needed to be successful.

Short tenures, broken spirits, dashed dreams, and even broken lives and families sometimes resulted from the sincere but frustrating experiences of those who had hoped to evangelize the world.

Phase III: Team Evangelism

I was at Abilene Christian College in 1953-1957, and I heard rousing speeches by returning missionaries about the need to go to the mission field with a team. The rhetoric made it sound like a team would be the panacea that would solve nearly all problems on the field and finally enable the church to carry out its mission to preach the gospel to the whole world. Our own missionary team formed on the Abilene campus in the spring of 1957 and left for Sao Paulo, Brazil, in South America on June 1, 1961. Earlier, a team from Abilene Christian College had moved to Austria with the hope of doing a work in Europe that would be dynamic and lasting.

Not only did groups form foreign mission work but also for the evangelization of the United States. We began to hear about exodus movements such as Exodus Bayshore, Exodus Rochester, and Exodus Burlington. Exodus movements took the idea of group or team evangelism and added to that concept the idea of vocational missionaries who would be self-supporting. Under this plan, one or more full-time workers would move into some city of the United States where the church was numerically small or nonexistent. A much larger contingency of members would move with the full-time workers and seek employment in schools, commerce, or industry and support themselves in the work of evangelizing the lost. Putting together the idea of team evangelism and self-supporting missionaries seemed to offer the perfect solution for two perplexing missionary problems: loneliness and lack of financial support.

Unfortunately, just going to the foreign field with the gospel did not resolve the problem of an unevangelized world, and team evangelism was not a perfect solution either. Going in a group was better than going alone, but the wise men among us had underestimated the difficult human relationships that would inevitably arise when men and women worked closely together under stressful conditions.

Satan is surely not going to fold his hands when a group of eager and committed young people move to town. He will simply work through the difficulties involved in interpersonal relationships and try to destroy the team from within. In every team I have ever known, getting along with fellow team members was the biggest single problem the group of missionaries faced. While team evangelism does to a great extent eliminate loneliness, it intensifies human relations problems.

In every team I have ever known, getting along with fellow team members was the biggest single problem the group of missionaries faced.

Exodus groups that moved to the northeastern part of the United States not only experienced human relations problems but also the difficulty of planting in the Northeast a church whose membership was largely Southern in customs, personality, and religious tradition. It was not uncommon to find dashed hopes and dreams within the exodus movements as sincere people awoke to the fact that internal strife among the members and external rejection by the community had produced few visible results after years and years of sacrificial effort. Team evangelism—the idea that had appeared to be the perfect solution for world evangelism—was not so perfect after all.

At some point during these years of searching for the perfect solution, certain educators with missionary backgrounds came to realize that besides team evangelism, missionaries needed special formal training in order to carry out their tasks. These brethren dedicated themselves, through additional training and private study, to the task of learning all they could from various denominations and our own experiences about successful missionary endeavors. The idea was that if we could learn the causes of failure and success in foreign mission efforts carried on by churches of Christ and other groups, we could teach proper methods in our courses and eliminate most of the problems faced by missionaries on the field.

Without doubt, the idea had merit. The truth is, however, that better education of missionaries has not enabled the church to arrive at a perfect solution for the difficulties that missionaries face. As one university administrator told me, "Although we have better missions education than we have ever had before, we have fewer people on the field now than before we started educating them. Further, some of those who went through our training program are not effective missionaries. Something is wrong."

One of the things wrong was that too much of the missionary methodology taught in the courses came from rural Third World settings and paid little attention to the urban environment to which so many of the church's missionaries go. What works in the African bush will not necessarily succeed in Sao Paulo, Brazil, a city of over 15 million inhabitants. It has taken a lot of us a long time to learn this lesson. When we should have focused our attention on missionary principles, some missions educators and missionaries were advocating a narrow set of methods that were supposed to work equally well all over the world. The trouble is, they didn't.

We can imagine, then, the frustration of well-educated missionary teams who followed the example of pioneer missionaries and went abroad to preach. They followed the examples of people like the Sao Paulo Missionary Team of 1961 and organized their own evangelistic teams to overcome loneliness and carry out an effective foreign missions effort. They sacrificed to get the best available missionary education from good schools. They went to the mission field and worked hard. Now, years later, they have very little to show for their efforts. What a frustration! They went in faith, overcame loneliness through team work, overcame ignorance through education, and church growth is still woefully slow.

It is only when we comprehend their frustration that we can understand why the Boston/Crossroads Movement has so much appeal to missionaries on the field.

Phase IV: The Discipling Movement

Discipling churches such as the Boston Church of Christ are also in search of the perfect solution for world missions. Some of the accomplishments of the Boston Church of Christ are impressive.

First, the church knows how to reach and teach the lost and their record of baptisms proves that they are evangelistic.

Second, the Boston church has a plan for evangelizing the world in this generation.[2]

Third, the Boston church is generous in its giving for world evangelism. In a special contribution at the Boston's World Mission Seminar in 1986, the church gave a total of over $1.8 million for missions. In 1987 at the same annual event, the church gave more than $3 million for world evangelism. The church's regular Sunday budget calls for a weekly contribution of $55,000.

Fourth, the Boston church has solved, for now at least, the problem of spending huge sums of money on real estate by renting the Boston Gardens for its weekly worship service. Weekday meetings are scattered throughout the Boston area in "house churches." Money that goes to pay mortgage installments in many churches can thus be directed into the church's main thrust, which is evangelism.

Fifth, the Boston church has shown remarkable success in producing leaders who are able to duplicate what is happening in Boston.

Sixth, the Boston church has been very effective in reaching and evangelizing highly capable young people and adults. They have learned to talk to the hearts and minds of hundreds of talented people who once were cold to the Christian faith and even today will pay no attention to mainline churches.

Conclusion

For those frustrated missionary men and women on distant fields around the world who have worked their hearts out and have few numerical results to show for the effort, news of the apparent success of discipling churches ignites again their dream that there may be a perfect solution for foreign missionary work.

Indeed, the six impressive accomplishments of the Boston church as listed above would make any missionary heart beat faster.

Unfortunately, there is a down side to the Boston church story. Discipling churches have not found the perfect missionary solution either. The next chapter will explain the inadequacies of the Boston/Crossroads approach to world missions.

NOTES FOR CHAPTER 6

[1]This statement appears at the bottom of a poster-photograph collection of pre-World War II missionaries. The poster is entitled "Churches of Christ

Missionary Portraiture" and was published December 30, 1926, by Don Carlos Janes of Louisville, Kentucky. It was in the Restoration Library Collection of Oklahoma Christian College.

[2]In the last section of this book, Gene Vinzant outlines what the Boston church and other discipling churches have done and plan to do in world evangelism.

CHAPTER

7

DISCIPLING CHURCHES: AN IMPERFECT MISSIONS SOLUTION

We saw in the previous chapter that churches and missionaries have searched throughout the years for the perfect solution to world evangelism. So far, they have been unsuccessful in their quest. We have never been able to reach the unevangelized fast enough and effectively enough to be satisfied with our efforts. Seldom can it be said of these efforts anywhere in the world that, like Paul and his comrades, we "have turned the world upside down" (Acts 17:6). In spite of thousands of inspirational speeches about going into all the world with the gospel of Jesus Christ, churches of Christ have not reached the world in our generation. Exciting rhetoric and high hopes have given way in some quarters to discouragement and disillusionment. Some churches and their leaders have given up entirely on the idea that an evangelized world is a possibility.

It is no wonder, then, that the impressive statistics amassed by discipling churches in the areas of conversion, retention, contribution for missions, and church planting have influenced other churches of Christ across the nation and around the world. We are a people who look for visible results from our evangelistic efforts. In far too many congregations, there have not been many visible results in recent years. Consequently, when word spreads that churches committed to a certain methodology are experiencing phenomenal numerical growth and have a plan to reach the whole world in this generation, brethren from all over the world search to find the reason for their success. In spite of periods of apathy, in our heart of hearts we are a brotherhood that longs to grow, that longs to succeed in evangelism, that longs to carry out the Great Commission.

Mood of Cautious Optimism

When word reached us about the growth rate in churches like the Crossroads Church of Christ in Gainesville, Florida, and the Boston Church of Christ in Boston, Massachusetts, we were curious. What were they doing right that so many of the rest of us were doing wrong? How was it that they were growing dramatically when others of our fellowship were experiencing little or no growth at all?

We then started hearing criticism. Since it is common to hear unsuccessful people criticize the successful ones in almost every endeavor, we suspected that there was a great deal of jealousy and envy in those who were negative about what the discipling churches were doing. At the same time, however, we heard very specific stories about some of the methods used by these brethren—stories that made us think the criticism might have some validity. We therefore adopted an attitude of "cautious optimism" about this fast-growing movement within churches of Christ.

As editor of the *Christian Chronicle,* an international newspaper of churches of Christ, I found myself facing a difficult question concerning how to report the results of brethren whose methodology was under heavy attack. I decided to treat this group as I would our mainline brethren and report their starting results. In response to some brethren who criticized the *Chronicle* for publicizing the efforts of discipling churches, I wrote an editorial in an attempt to explain why we continued to cover the work of the Boston/Crossroads churches. In that editorial, I explained that the *Christian Chronicle* reports news about the discipling churches because we believe that they are our brethren and their actions are newsworthy. I then went on to explain

> This does not mean that we agree with everything they do. We have serious questions about what we understand to be their definition of fruit bearing, the demands they make on their members, their leadership patterns, their insistence that their way is *the* way to evangelize, their tendency to believe that they are the faithful remnant while the rest of us are deadwood and their studied isolation from the brotherhood at large. . . . No, we do not approve of everything we hear about the Boston/Crossroads churches. Mentioning them in our news columns is not endorsement of all their method.[1]

I did not intend for that editorial to be a pro-discipling movement statement. Rather, I thought it was an article that would point out some genuine concerns about the movement and, at the same time, would call brethren of good will in mainline congregations not to rush to judgment and sever relations with these brethren of suspicious methodology whose visible results seemed so impressive.

As the months went by. I discovered more and more brethren both in the United States and in foreign countries who felt that the editorial had indeed endorsed the discipling methodology. They regarded the *Chronicle* and its editor as pro-Boston/Crossroads. I still do not understand how people arrived at that conclusion from the editorial. Whether their conclusion was due to my inability to articulate concerns or to their reading into the editorial what they wanted to see, I want to state clearly here and now that I was always "cautiously optimistic"—only that and nothing more. I was never pro-Boston. There were always deep concerns that the critics of the movement might be right. I just wanted the brotherhood to be careful in its judgment and not adopt an attitude toward these zealous brethren that would preclude the possibility of unity and peace in the body of Christ.

Cautious Optimism Gives Way to Pessimism

As the months passed after the appearance of that editorial, I became more and more concerned about the direction being taken by the discipling churches. Finally, I decided to publish a second editorial that would spell out more clearly some of my principle fears about the movement. In that editorial, I outlined three major objections.

> First and foremost, the Boston/Crossroads churches take away individual Christian liberty from their members. They do this by speaking where the Bible does not speak and binding man made religious laws on people who should be free in Christ. The leaders of this type of congregation believe that they have the right to go beyond the Scriptures and create commandments that members must follow.
>
> If the members protest these human laws, they pay the consequences. They are shamed, shunned and either forced into line or forced out of the fellowship. While we also believe in church discipline, we believe that withdrawal of fellowship must be based exclusively on God's law—not man's. . . .
>
> A second serious error of the Boston/Crossroads movement is its system of leadership. It is built on authority, power and intimidation. The leaders (or leader) at the top of the authority pyramid in the local con-

> gregation demand submission and obedience from their followers. Each member has a person who is over him or her in a supervisory position, and each member is accountable to his or her supervisor/discipler. A doctrine of submission holds the pyramid together. At the very top of the congregational pyramid of authority and power, one or two people gain mastery over the entire congregation. . . .
>
> A third serious error of the Boston/Crossroads movement is that it is inherently divisive. Personal conversation with one of the leaders of this movement has convinced me that this divisiveness begins in the heart because these brethren do not really believe that there are any faithful churches except the ones in their sphere of influence. They consider themselves to be "the faithful remnant." The rest of us—regardless of the work we have done, the results achieved and the years dedicated to the cause of Christ—are apparently considered unfruitful, lukewarm or dead. The Boston/Crossroads leaders have drawn a circle to keep out anyone who has not submitted to their philosophy and method.
>
> The divisiveness continues when leaders of this movement decide to plant a church in a new area of the world. They convince some faithful worker, who has been groomed for years to be a church leader, that he is really wasting his time and talent working among the "lukewarm" or "dead" churches where he himself was born again. Through heavy doses of guilt and a steady stream of discouraging words, the Boston/Crossroads movement persuades church leaders in the United States and abroad to train at one of their bases like Boston or New York for two years and then sends them out to plant a church that siphons off members of churches already planted.[2]

There is an obvious change in tone between the first and the second editorials. What provoked this move toward pessimism concerning the discipling churches?

Reasons for Change in Attitude

Shortly after the first editorial appeared, I had a lengthy conversation in May 1986 with a missionary in South America who advocated the discipling methodology. I advised him that he needed to take great care in dealing with this group on the mission field because of the long history of church divisions associated with the implementation of that methodology. His response was, "Well, I think there may be times when a local church needs to divide if the church is so dead that it is not growing." This frightened me because he was talking so casually about what should happen to churches in which my friends and I had dedicated many years of our lives. We knew those churches were not perfect, but we did not believe division would cure spiritual problems. His careless approach to the idea of church division caused flags to go up in my mind.

Not long after that conversation, I was in Lisbon, Portugal, for an evangelistic campaign in June 1986. At the time, and I believe this is still true at the time of this writing, the church in Lisbon was the fastest-growing church of Christ on the European continent in terms of the number of full-time workers involved in the effort. We were in the midst of a marvelous campaign when I found out that one of the team members was considering leaving Lisbon in order to train in Boston or New York and then come back to establish a completely new work in Lisbon.

As different ones probed this missionary's desire to leave Lisbon, train in Boston, and return to establish a new congregation, the story emerged that church leaders in Boston and New York had contacted him and encouraged him to take this step. I have since been told by one of the New York leaders that the missionary first contacted them about training him. I do not know which story is correct. I do know that a common tactic in the discipling churches is to criticize any work that is not theirs and discourage people about the training and work they have done with mainline churches of Christ. It is no wonder, therefore, that people who leave the discipling churches often leave the church entirely. They receive a steady diet of what is wrong with all churches of Christ except the discipling churches. When they reach a dead end with the discipling group that is supposed to be so good and effective, they often see no need to attend a mainline church of Christ that they had been constantly warned to avoid.

It is no wonder, therefore, that people who leave the discipling churches often leave the church entirely.

The Lisbon missionary was so discouraged about the highly successful work in which he was engaged that he was ready to leave his beloved co-worker by himself and seek the perfect missionary solution in New York. Fortunately, good brethren warned him against this approach, and he listened to them. He continues to do outstanding evangelistic work in Lisbon, Portugal.

In the fall of 1986, I learned that there had been a serious division in one of the congregations in Sao Paulo, Brazil. It was the church where the future New York missionary team had worshipped from May through August of 1986 while doing a language and cultural training internship prior to moving permanently to Sao Paulo to begin mission work in 1987. I was very worried about plans of the New York church to send a missionary team into Sao Paulo, the city where my wife and I had lived with our family for some 16 years. When we arrived in Sao Paulo in 1961 with 12 other families, there were two tiny congregations in that city. By 1987, there were 17 or 18 congregations. I was anxious about the negative effect the New York team would have on the churches our team had helped establish and train.

When I learned in May of 1986 that one of my missionary friends had agreed to help the New York group set up their language and cultural classes and serve as a kind of host to the group, I was relieved. I felt that the missionary who stepped forward to help out in this way would be extremely careful about their doctrine and methodology and would unhesitatingly rebuke them if they got out of line. What happened, however, was that he liked a great deal of what he saw. According to two key leaders of the Santana congregation, their members began to feel pressure from the missionary while the New York group was in its training program. When the New York group returned to the United States in August of 1986, the two leaders affirm that the missionary began to utilize an authoritarian approach. The members rebelled and requested the American missionary, his family, and their followers to leave the congregation and not come back. In other words, the Brazilian brethren withdrew fellowship from those believed to be sympathizers of the discipling movement.

That action sent a shock wave through churches of Christ all over Brazil. While I had expected a division like this to occur at some point because of the influence of the New York methodology, I never dreamed it would happen so quickly. This division took place in October of 1986. In fairness to the missionary who is, and always will be, a beloved brother, I do not believe he would have accepted the methodology had he witnessed its full cycle. He was impressed by the early stages of the technique and never had a chance to see the whole approach in action.

In November of 1986 at the Pan American Lectureship in Mexico City, a group of us from mainline congregations and from discipling churches met for lunch and discussion. Those present were Al Baird, elder of the Boston church; Andy Lindo, a leader of the Boston church; John Bailey, an elder of the Pipeline Road church in Hurst, Texas; Dale Brown, now an elder of the Golf Course Road church in Midland, Texas; Teston Gilpatrick, a missionary to Sao Paulo, Brazil; and Howard Norton. Our conversation was good, and it was frank. We all asked questions of one another, debated critical issues, and, I believe, left as friends. We continue to be friends and brothers to this day.

I came away from that meeting, however, convinced that the leadership of the discipling churches was committed to the view that it had the right to make religious demands on members that God himself had not made. I came away fully convinced that the leadership did not believe in the restoration principle of "speak where the Bible speaks and be silent where the Bible is silent." On the contrary, this group believed that it had the right to speak for God, make rules for its members that God had not made, and hold members accountable for obeying those human commandments.

As I learned at a later meeting in Boston—in the spring of 1987, a meeting between our mainline church leaders and four of the discipling movement leaders—the Boston leaders based their "right" to make religious rules that God had not made on this premise: "Fathers have the right to make rules for their children that God did not make, and children who disobey those rules sin against God just as surely as if God himself had made the rules. The church is more important than the family, and elders have the responsibility for leading the church. Elders, therefore, have the right to bind rules on members that God did not bind. Those who disobey the elders' rules sin against God just as surely as if God himself had made the rules."

Once the full impact of this kind of fallacious logic sank into my mind, I knew that I was going to have to speak against these precepts and not be silent.

In December of 1986, the elders of the Memorial Church of Christ in Houston, Texas, asked me to fly to Houston and talk with them about the dangers facing the churches of Christ in Sao Paulo because of the projected New York church planting there. The Memorial church had invested money and energy during a timespan of some 25 years. They had fully supported Brazilian evangelist Modesto Pellegrini and me for several of those years. Out of that meeting came an invitation for Don Vinzant and me to travel to Sao Paulo and warn the brethren concerning the dangers we believed they would be facing once the New York missionary team arrived permanently in the city.

I was glad that Memorial wanted both Don and me to make the difficult trip since he and I, along with our wives, were the ones who started the Sao Paulo Missionary Team that went to Brazil in 1961. The things we learned and experienced during that trip to Sao Paulo just after Christmas of 1986 and in the first few days of 1987—plus the information we have continued to glean since our return to the United States—have made it clear to me that virtually every doubt or fear I ever entertained about the discipling churches is justified.

The Sao Paulo Experience

Relying on information we had gleaned over many months and in consultation with brethren in the United States, we decided to divide our Brazil effort into two parts and deal with the discipling movement head-on. First, we decided to conduct a seminar for church leaders in Sao Paulo entitled, "A Study Concerning Our Freedom in Christ." Secondly, we determined to follow up the seminar presentation by contacting personally as many Brazilian and American church leaders in Brazil as we could to prepare them for what we thought they would have to face in the days ahead. The plan worked well.

The Seminar

Invitations went out to church leaders all over Sao

Paulo and to some parts of the Brazilian Interior. All in all, we spent about 10 hours in serious public study and discussion. The schedule was as follows:

Friday,

8:00 p.m.—"Why We Are Here"—Howard Norton

8:30 p.m.—"A Biblical Study of What Paul Says Concerning Our Freedom in Christ"—Don Vinzant

9:15 p.m.—"The New York Church and Christian Liberty"—Howard Norton

10:00 p.m.—Discussion—Don Vinzant

Saturday,

10:00 a.m.—"A Biblical Study of What Paul Says Concerning Our Freedom in Christ" (2)—Don Vinzant

10:45 a.m.—"The New York Church and Christian Liberty" (2)—Howard Norton

11:45 a.m.—"Is the New York Church a Cult?"—Howard Norton

12:15 p.m.—Discussion—Don Vinzant

12:45 p.m.—"The Future of the Church of Christ in Brazil"—Howard Norton

2:30 p.m.—Discussion and Plans for the Future—Don Vinzant

We felt that the presentation entitled "Why We Are Here" was very important for the approximately 75 people who were present on Friday night. We explained that we were there because we felt an obligation to let Brazilian Christians know that the New York group that planned to move into Sao Paulo was not like any other group of American Christians whom we had recommended to them in the past. Brazilians had always accepted complete strangers whom we recommended and asked no questions. We explained that we could not conscientiously recommend this group of people because we felt that they used methods that were contrary to Scripture and contrary to the spirit of Brazilian democracy and freedom.

We explained that we were there because we felt an obligation to let Brazilian Christians know that the New York group that planned to move into Sao Paulo was not like any other group of American Christians whom we had recommended to them in the past.

We further explained that groups of this kind were not welcome to practice their methods on some of our American Christian college campuses, that some of our very best elderships strongly opposed their approach to the Lord's work, and that some of our most respected opinion leaders in the church strongly objected to the extremes that characterized their methods.

We explained that we were present to strengthen those brethren and congregations who had been so badly shaken by the church problems that had come to a head in October of 1986 with the disfellowship proceedings of the Santana church. The division in Santana was the first such happening in a Sao Paulo church in the 30-year history of churches of Christ in that metropolis. The events at Santana had also severely affected two or three other churches in the area. Besides this, the Ninth of July church had almost experienced a division because certain brethren there had tried to use authoritarian techniques on members in that congregation—the only church of Christ in Brazil with elders and deacons.

We explained that we did not want to see another Jim Jones situation in South America. While we did not believe, nor do we believe, that there is anyone in the discipling churches with the immediate tendencies of a Jim Jones in Guyana, we said that we believed that movements like the one we were discussing could easily degenerate into that kind of a movement because the effectiveness of the movement required total submission to those in charge.

We reminded the brethren of the importance of our freedom in Christ. We know that they were happy to have escaped Catholicism, Pentecostalism, and Protestantism and the man-made laws under which they had once lived in those religious systems. We urged them never to let anyone persuade them to go back into such bondage to man-made rules but rather to be true to the principle of speaking where the Bible speaks and being silent where the Bible is silent.

We told them that we wanted our visit to help restore the unity and love among Sao Paulo brethren that had been there since 1956, that we wanted to help them develop a plan for confronting this erroneous approach to evangelism, and that we wanted to urge Sao Paulo churches to become ever more evangelistic in their local congregations.

Don Vinzant and I divided the seminar itself into two parts. Vinzant taught material entitled "A Biblical Study of What Paul Says Concerning Our Freedom in Christ." He dealt especially with teachings on Christian liberty in Galatians and Colossians. He showed that the binding of human opinions on Christians, regardless of how noble the goal that such rules are designed to attain, is patently false from a biblical standpoint. Showing that Christian liberty is one of our most precious spiritual blessings, he warned against any movement, inside or outside the church, that seeks to limit one's liberty in Christ.

. . . the binding of human opinions on Christians, regardless of how noble the goal that such rules are designed to attain, is patently false from a biblical standpoint.

Perhaps the greatest contribution Vinzant made, however, was to point out that authoritarian movements within Christianity are not new. He even suggested that our discipling brethren might have learned their authoritarian approach from groups completely outside the Restoration Movement. As he demonstrates in another part of this book, the charismatic movement was shot through with authoritarianism for a number of years. Vinzant raised this question concerning where the leaders of the discipling movement discovered the principles they now use. These principles, he said, almost always have their parallel in other authoritarian Christian movements and in the practice of cults. If power and intimidation are not acceptable methods when we view them in certain parts of the charismatic movement and in various cults, then power and intimidation are not acceptable for use in any church of Christ no matter how noble the goal that we are attempting to reach through the use of such methods.

In my part of the seminar, I listed eight objections to the methodology of the discipling churches and their leaders. First, discipling methodology enslaves church members by taking away their freedom to make their own choices in those areas where the Bible does not speak. Just as a Roman Catholic bishop does not have the right to make one single religious rule for members to obey, the leaders in churches of Christ have no right to make one religious rule and bind it on the members. Their doctrine of submission to disciplers and other leaders, their doctrine of confessing sins to the discipler, their pressure on members to use their time and run their private lives the way the leaders want them to (or suffer the rejection of "friends"), their unwillingness to baptize believers until they agree to follow the human directives of the leaders, and their creation of a kind of perpetual dependency on the leaders of the church all lead to a frightening loss of freedom in Christ. It is a loss that no Christian should ever agree to experience.

> . . . discipling methodology enslaves church members by taking away their freedom to make their own choices in those areas where the Bible does not speak.

Second, the methodology of the discipling churches causes division within the body of Christ. Their doctrine of the "faithful remnant" cannot but cause division. Although some leaders deny the teaching of this doctrine, they believe that *they* are the faithful remnant. Other churches of Christ, virtually without exception, are either lukewarm or dead. They do not have God's blessings or they would be growing at the rate acceptable to the leaders of authoritarian churches. Discipling churches are growing. They therefore reason that God is blessing them. People in lukewarm or dead churches should get out of them, move to a discipling church, be discipled by someone there, and then do an effective work for God. There is no room in discipling churches for weak members. It is a movement designed to accommodate the drives of supermen and superwomen. Those whose energy and interest levels do not measure up to the ever-increasing standards of the leaders must either get with the program or move out of the way.

Third, the movement exalts leaders to the position of dictators. Leaders say that they welcome the reasonings of those who disagree with the leadership. The truth, however, is that those who continue to ask questions because they continue to disagree are viewed as prideful and of a bad heart. Submission and loyalty are the currency of the realm. People who ask too many questions are considered insubordinate, disloyal, and full of human pride. Leaders must be obeyed. Followers must submit blindly to their direction.

Fourth, the discipling churches have a weak doctrine

of grace. Disciplers take a legalistic approach to spiritual growth. Instead of merely instilling inspiration and principles of the spiritual life in members so that they can use them in their own development, Christian growth becomes a kind of "forced feeding." Disciplers ask questions like, Did you read your Bible today? Did you talk to someone today about his salvation? Did you pray today? Why weren't you at the Friday night Bible study? You say you were sick, but why didn't you rise above it and come anyway? Advice must be taken. The mood is, "If you don't take my advice, I won't put up with you anymore."

. . . the discipling churches have a weak doctrine of grace.

Guilt is an important part of the methodology. Leaders and disciplers make the rules, quiz the members to see if they are keeping the man-made ordinances, criticize them when they do not, view them as prideful sinners,and eventually shun them if they choose not to submit to the opinions of those in charge.

Leaders and disciplers make the rules, quiz the members to see if they are keeping the man-made ordinances, criticize them when they do not, view them as prideful sinners, and eventually shun them if they choose not to submit to the opinions of those in charge.

In the bulletin of the Boston Church of Christ for August 17, 1986, Ed Townsend had an article with the title "Because You Say So." In this article he used the example of Peter letting down the nets in the deep water just because Jesus said so, even though they had worked all night without catching anything. He argued that Christians must submit to their disciplers in the same way Peter submitted to Jesus: totally, unconditionally, without question. Although I did not have this article at the time of the seminar, it illustrates the kind of control that leaders expect to exercise over their followers.

Fifth, the discipling churches have a weak doctrine of church growth. Whereas 1 Corinthians 3:6 shows that God is responsible for growth, these brethren leave the impression that if everyone will just work hard enough with the correct methodology, ministers can make church growth happen. Workers who are not producing must be doing something wrong, and churches that are not growing at the rate the leaders determine as the norm are either lukewarm or dead.

The truth, however, is that God does not hold us personally responsible for church growth. He holds us personally responsible for faithfulness to the task of preaching. Effective evangelism does not always produce impressive results, as Paul's visit to Mars Hill and Christ's teaching in Nazareth clearly demonstrate.

God does not hold us personally responsible for church growth. He holds us personally responsible for faithfulness to the task of preaching.

Sixth, discipling churches have a weak doctrine of gifts and ministries. Paul explains in 1 Corinthians 12-14 that we do not all have the same gift. These brethren, however, attempt to push everyone into the same mold and force them into situations and types of behavior that quite often do not fit the talents and personalities of the members. Winning people to Christ, in the view of many of these brethren, is the only valid test of a worker's faithfulness.

Seventh, discipling churches use a methodology for evangelism and edification that can be psychologically damaging. The material in this book by Flavil Yeakley, Jr. goes into great detail about this particular abuse. Every reader should carefully study his findings.

Eighth, discipling churches employ methods that are similar to those used by harmful cults in American society. Is this movement a cult? I do not know. I do know from talking to people who have come out of the movement and to those who have worked closely with people in the movement that the discipling churches are cult-like and that they do gain a kind of mind control over the members. The movement has a hypnotic effect on its members. This kind of control is not normally found in churches of Christ nor in any of their members' para-church institutions. Any person who is in a discipling church should read some good articles on how cults function. If he finds a cluster of cult-like characteristics in the church he attends, he should remove himself from that congregation and seek the fellowship of a more balanced church of Christ.

These eight objectives would grow to twelve if I were giving the seminar today. The other four objectives would be as follows:

(1) Members who were baptized without a total commitment to submit to their disciplers are now being re-immersed in significant numbers. Even respected church leaders among the discipling churches are being re-immersed.

(2) The Boston church is taking charge of local churches in different parts of America. It is the "Mother Church" that tells other churches what to do.

(3) The authority of the evangelist is growing to the point that the primary evangelist of the Boston church tells evangelists in other churches what to do. Some people think he tells the Boston elders what to do, also. They deny this, however.

The authority of the evangelist is growing to the point that the primary evangelist of the Boston church tells evangelists in other churches what to do.

---

(4) There is a growing tendency for these brethren to use the allegorical approach in the interpretation of Scripture. With this treatment of the text, one can make a text mean whatever he wants it to mean.

What To Do?

People on the mission fields of the world, especially in metropolitan areas, will probably have to deal with the discipling movement sometime in the near future. What can missionaries do when they realize that a discipling church planting is going to take place in the city or region where they work? The answer is not easy, and I do not claim to have the infallible response to the question. I do, however, have twelve suggestions. Let me list these and comment briefly on each one.

First, develop a strategy for dealing with these brethren before the matter becomes an issue where you are. There are now enough good brethren with experience in facing the problem that there is no reason for any watchman to be caught by surprise and without adequate information when the authoritarian group arrives.

Second, remember that these brethren of the discipling churches are reacting against evangelistic apathy in other churches of Christ. While you cannot neglect a good defense against their errors, a strong evangelistic work in your own congregation is one of the most effective ways to stand against their aggressive tactics.

Third, remember that these men and women are our brethren. We can resist their false teaching and their dangerous methodology without jumping to the conclusion that there must be an immediate and permanent rupture in our relationship with them. I personally like most of these brethren whom I have met. They are zealous and sincere. I want to learn to be as zealous for the lost as they are, but I want to teach them the way of the Lord more perfectly. I want us all to be united in Christ "for we be brethren."

Fourth, keep yourself pure. Our battle is not against flesh and blood, and we must not approach our struggle with them in a carnal way. If we adopt the methods of Satan or the methods of sinful man to fight a spiritual battle, the cause of Christ will suffer untold damage.

Fifth, prepare the brethren in your area before this movement arrives. If the Sao Paulo seminar and private conversation approach will not work in your area, find something that will. Do not leave those in your charge without instruction and warning. No one but you can adequately handle this responsibility.

Sixth, confront the discipling people when they arrive in your area. Tell them that you consider them brethren but brethren who are dangerous to the work you are trying to do. Let them know in no uncertain terms that you will not tolerate any abuse of the people whom God has given you to lead and protect.

Seventh, pray that these brethren will not complicate your own immigrant status with the government where you are living. Those working with visas in Brazil believe that these documents are becoming harder and harder to arrange because of some highly questionable methods that they believe were used by the New York team in order to get into the country over the objection of local Brazilian church leaders.

Eighth, if you do not want this group to work in your city, write their elders and plead with them not to come.

This may not resolve anything, but the elders need to know your sentiments and those of other brethren who have been serving in that city over a period of years.

Ninth, pray that all of us can make enough changes within the will of God that we can work together in peace. Pray that a spirit of love and unity may permeate every worker in your city so that people will believe that God sent Jesus and that He loves us.

Tenth, revitalize your own congregation. If it is lukewarm, if it is dead, deal with it. Try to correct it. Ask God to give you the strength and wisdom to turn your work into a dynamic force for good that will bring glory to the name of Almighty God.

Eleventh, develop a ministry for caring for those who drop out of the discipling church. I am told by a responsible source that there is a flow of people leaving the Boston church. Such people need loving, tender care in order to overcome the scars and bruises that they sustain within the discipling movement.

Twelfth, keep reaching out to these brethren who are caught up in the enthusiasm and false hope that they have found the perfect missionary solution. Most of these brethren, I am convinced, want to please and glorify God. In spite of their dedication, they are on a path that leads to burn-out and spiritual disillusionment. While we do not approve of their tactics, they are nevertheless brethren for whom Christ died. Let us always treat them with the same love and respect that we desire for ourselves.

NOTES FOR CHAPTER 7

[1]"What about News from Boston?" *Christian Chronicle,* April 1986.
[2]"Second Thoughts on Boston," *Christian Chronicle,* February 1987.

PART III

HISTORICAL ROOTS OF THE DISCIPLING MOVEMENT AMONG CHURCHES OF CHRIST

by Don Vinzant

ABOUT THE AUTHOR

Don E. Vinzant has served as the pulpit minister of the Grandbury Church of Christ in Grandbury, Texas, since 1982. Before that, he preached for the Northside Church of Christ in Austin, Texas, 1976–1982, and for the Village (now Quail Springs) Church of Christ in Oklahoma City, 1973–1976. He was on the original Sao Paulo Mission Team, 1961–1973. He served as the dean of the Sao Paulo Institute of Biblical Studies, 1970–1973.

He contributed chapters to *Steps to the Mission Field,* a mission textbook. He translated works of Rubem Alves, Brazil's leading Protestant theologian/philosopher. In addition, he has published numerous articles in various religious journals.

Don received his B.A. degree from Abilene Christian University in 1958, his M.A. degree from Abilene Christian University in 1962, and his D. Min. degree from Austin Presbyterian Theological Seminary in 1984.

CHAPTER

8

ROOTS OF THE MODERN DISCIPLING MOVEMENT

Disciples need to be called Christians again. It happened first in Antioch (Acts 11:26) and it needs to happen today. The words "disciple," "discipling," and "discipleship" have been so abused that they no longer communicate what they used to. The terms may some day be rescued and used again in the biblical sense. For now, however, other terms used in the New Testament for Christian growth will serve much better.

Where did the modern authoritarian discipling system come from? Who dreamed up this pyramid scheme of a young evangelist controlling the lives of converts so that they grind out huge work quotas and big number baptisms? What are the roots of this system?

This particular form of authoritarianism largely ran its course in other religious groups and has been abandoned. There is a large body of literature full of warnings and criticism of this authoritarianism as it has been tried by others. The fact that it has been tried by others is rather embarrassing to those who thought that someone in the churches of Christ invented this approach. The reality, however, is that churches of Christ are among the last ones to be damaged by the discipling movement.

This particular form of authoritarianism largely ran its course in other religious groups and has been abandoned.

A Search for Roots

As the following diagram suggests, there are five important roots of the modern discipling movement as it now appears among churches of Christ. Each of these roots will be considered in this chapter. Chapter Nine presents criticism of the discipling movement as it appeared in other religious groups. Statements from many religious leaders explain why they rejected the discipling approach.

The first root of the modern discipling movement may be found in the Roman Catholic Spiritual Directors of the fifth century and later throughout Roman Catholic history. The Spiritual Director system operated in monasteries and convents for many centuries. Those being trained were told to reveal their most secret thoughts to their Spiritual Director and submit themselves totally to their Spiritual director's decisions as to what is good and evil. This is essentially what is now called a "discipling relationship." The idea of confessing sins to a discipler obviously comes from the Catholic tradition and their doctrine of auricular confession. Because of abuses, the Roman Catholic Church built in a safeguard in their Spiritual Director arrangement. They found that personal domination and manipulation can easily run out of control when one person is both the confessor and the Spiritual Director. They began to require, therefore, that the confessor and the Spiritual Director could not be the same person. In this regard, the modern discipling movement is about where the Roman Catholic Church was almost 1,500 years ago. They have not yet learned the danger of having one

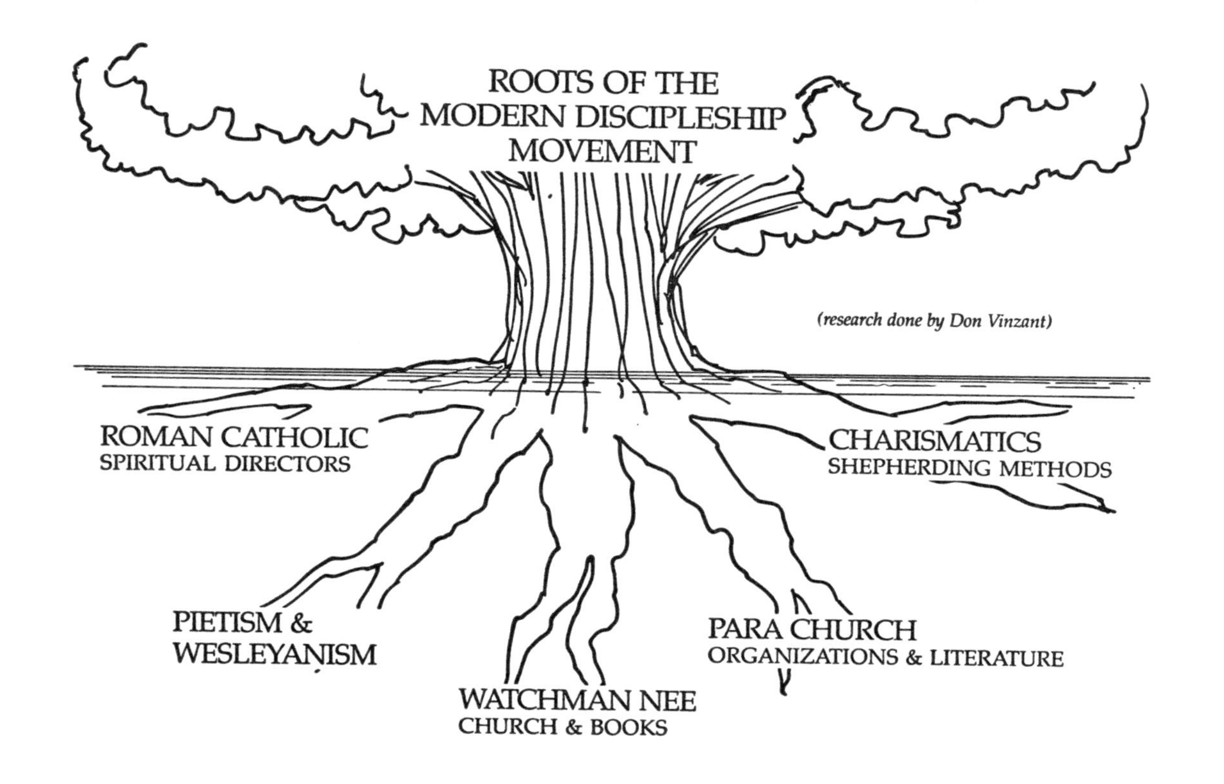
ROOTS OF THE
MODERN DISCIPLESHIP
MOVEMENT
(research done by Don Vinzant)
ROMAN CATHOLIC
SPIRITUAL DIRECTORS
CHARISMATICS
SHEPHERDING METHODS
PIETISM &
WESLEYANISM
PARA CHURCH
ORGANIZATIONS & LITERATURE
WATCHMAN NEE
CHURCH & BOOKS

person serve both as the confessor and the Spiritual Director for another person.[1]

Those being trained were told to reveal their most secret thoughts to their Spiritual Director and submit themselves totally to their Spiritual director's decisions as to what is good and evil.

In the Roman Catholic Church today there is much less emphasis on each person having a Spiritual Director and more emphasis on each person having spiritual direction. Based on his work with the Association for Psychological Type, Flavil Yeakley reports that the Roman Catholic Church was the first religious group to make widespread use of Jungian typology, the Myers-Briggs Type Indicator, and other approaches to personality differences as a way of counseling individuals about the spiritual direction their lives should take. They now clearly recognize the value of diversity and do not try to make members over after the image of the group norm.

Pietism/Wesleyanism

A second root of the discipling movement is to be found in Pietism/Wesleyanism. Early in the Reformation, such men as Spener, Franke, and Zinzendorf wanted to breathe new life into ice cold state churches. John Wesley was impressed by Spener's use of small groups *(collegia pietatis)* for this purpose. This influenced him to establish Methodist societies within Anglican churches. These small groups soon came to see themselves as a church within a church. They believed that they had achieved a higher level of spirituality than that experienced by other Christians.

Eventually they broke with the Anglican fellowship and became a separate denomination.

This is similar to what happened when Crossroads-trained campus ministers went into churches of Christ throughout the nation and started using the discipling approach. The "Soul Talk" group became a church within a church. Those involved in using this approach saw themselves as being superior to the "lukewarm" or "dead" members who were not involved in the discipling ministry. They thought of themselves as being the "faithful remnant." They sought perfection through rule-keeping and thus demonstrated pietistic tendencies toward legalism. Such a spirit leads to divisiveness. It produces end-runs around good elders. It tempts toward elitism and a kind of self-importance. Study Pietism and you will find an important source of much that characterizes the discipling movement.[2]

Watchman Nee

A third root of the authoritarian approach to discipling can be found in the writings and influence of Watchman Nee. He is the favorite theologian of many modern charismatics. Nee is a somewhat heroic figure because he suffered a long imprisonment by the Chinese Communists. In his early career, he went through a brief association with the Plymouth Brethren and came under the influence of Pietism. In later years, he advocated very forcefully a strong role for those with "delegated authority." As Russell T. Hitt reported,

> Watchman Nee, a prolific writer and leader of the indigenous Chinese church movement known as the Little Flock, makes a strong plea for the need for Christians to obey delegated authority in the church. "The church is a place not only for fellowship of brothers and sisters," says Nee, "but also for the manifestation of authority."[3]

Nee's writings on spiritual authority and on the normal church life reflect the kind of Asian authoritarianism that prevailed before World War II. According to Bob Buess, Nee required blanket obedience regardless of morals or righteousness simply for the sake of obedience.[4]

Nee taught that each person must have a "covering" in the Lord. He used that term for a person who has delegated authority, who must be obeyed unconditionally, and who must be imitated. He also taught that Christians must confess their sins to the person who is their "covering." Jerram Barrs explained that the doctrine of "covering" means that ideas, decisions, and lifestyle must be covered by someone higher in the chain of command; thus the "covering" gives instructions on many secular matters and not just on matters of faith.[5] This, of course, is what the discipling churches such as the Boston Church of Christ call a "discipler."

Nee had another doctrine that has been picked up by the Boston Church of Christ. He taught that there should be only one congregation in each city. Juan Carlos Ortiz later advocated the same thing. When Nee's "Little Flock" moved into a city, they proclaimed themselves as the only church (and the only local congregation) approved by God in that city. Study the writings of Watchman Nee and you will find that the discipling movement did not begin with the Boston Church of Christ or the Crossroads Church of Christ. It did not begin with Kip McKean or Chuck Lucas. It did not begin in churches of Christ at all.

Parachurch Organizations

A fourth root of the discipling movement is found in certain parachurch organizations. The term "parachurch" is applied to evangelical organizations with no church affiliation or sponsorship. Two parachurch organizations helped shape the discipling movement.

In 1934, Dawson Trotman founded a parachurch organization known as the "Navigators." Trotman, a strong leader and a true evangelistic entrepreneur, is remembered as having a somewhat authoritarian and dogmatic style. He ran a tight ship and was often confrontational and abrupt with those who worked under him. He would assign workers to any geographic location as it occurred to him. He often had Navigator "houses" where a number of Navigators would share living quarters—with no hint, however, of any moral improperties. The kind of one-on-one follow-up after conversion that Trotman taught was very similar to the discipling approach practiced by the Boston Church of Christ and other discipling churches.[6]

Since Trotman's death, his successor, Lorne Sanny, has adopted a modified leadership style. A journal published by the Navigators recently warned against the abuse of discipling relationships. The article warned about authoritarian intervention into the private life of the one being discipled. The article suggested that such a practice can foster over-dependency in the recipient and furnish unhealthy ego-gratification for the discipler.[7]

Another parachurch organization that influenced the discipling movement is a group known as "Campus Crusade." Bill and Vonette Bright are its leaders. They are as cheerful and sunny as their last name suggests. Bill has been in campus work for almost four decades. Campus Crusade has led the way among evangelical fundamentalists in several areas.

Historian Richard Quebedeaux observed that Bright is an authoritarian leader with a chain of command placing himself clearly at the top as leader of Campus Crusade. Further, he says, there is a lack of any effective self-criticism within the organization. Concerning Bright, Quebedaux adds, ". . . it has been very difficult for him to divorce himself from the pietistic tendencies toward legalism and super-spirituality, despite his words to the contrary."[8] It should be noted that this criticism comes in a work about Bright and Campus Crusade that is highly favorable. Similar criticisms have been made concerning the leaders of the discipling movement among churches of Christ.

The Charismatic Movement

The last root of the discipling movement as it has appeared among churches of Christ is seen in the charismatic movement. This movement developed outside traditional denominational structures. Similar doctrines had been taught earlier in Pentecostal denominations such as the Assemblies of God, the Church of God, and the Pentecostal Holiness Church. In the late 1950s, however, a Neo-Pentecostal charismatic movement began. There was no structure to this growing movement. To this loose and amorphous group came five men offering leadership with a capital "L." They were known as the Shepherds of Fort Lauderdale, Florida. These five leaders were Don Basham, Ern Baxter, Bob Mumford, Derek Prince, and Charles Simpson. These men formed the "Holy Spirit Teaching Mission," later renamed "Christian Growth Ministries." They began producing tapes, books, and a monthly magazine called *New Wine*.

A 1975 article in *Christianity Today* discussed problems that followed in the wake of the new charismatic shepherding movement.

> A dispute is taking place over issues of authority and discipleship. Powerful figures in the movement have built up a chain of command linking many local groups around the country to themselves. . . . Discipleship involves submission to the shepherd as he points the way—and points out flaws in behavior. . . . Some travel to Ft. Lauderdale to receive training directly from Mumford and his colleagues. . . . Those being

> discipled must consult with their shepherd about many personal decisions. In some cases, shepherds forbid marriages, reject school and vocational plans, demand confession of secret sins. . . .[9]

The five Shepherds of Fort Lauderdale taught and practiced a style of leadership that they called "shepherding." They used this term to describe attempts to control the private lives of their members. In 1972, shortly after they added the authoritarian tone to their teaching, Juan Carlos Ortiz came from Argentina to Fort Lauderdale. His presentations in Fort Lauderdale had wide reception—including some from the churches of Christ. Ortiz taught the same thing as Watchman Nee about one congregation to a city. He also taught authoritarianism to the point that he said disciples should be told which individuals they should take home with them for meals.[10]

Russell Hitt's article on the top religious news events of 1975 went beyond the discussion of Watchman Nee that was mentioned earlier. That article also discussed problems with the shepherding movement.

> The charismatic movement's oneness in the Spirit has been badly strained by a disagreement on the nature and methods of discipleship training between Bob Mumford of Christian Growth Ministries, Fort Lauderdale, Florida, and a variety of charismatic VIPs. . . . Mumford is charged with constructing an overly rigid, denomination-like hierarchy of "shepherds" whose spiritual authority over their charges is called a threat to . . . the interdenominational character of the charismatic movement itself. Mumford denies wanting to form a new denomination, but his opponents so far haven't had ears to hear.[11]

Bob Buess attributes many of these problems in the shepherding movement to the influence of Juan Carlos Ortiz. In his book *Discipleship Pro and Con,* he wrote,

> Juan Carlos Ortiz came from Argentina to America and is now traveling in various parts of the world spreading his version of discipleship. . . . The shepherd is treated like an earthly father would be treated. . . . In neo-discipleship groups there is absolute submision to the shepherd. Everyone is submitted in a regimented (army type) authoritarian chain of command. . . . Someone is between you and God at all times.[12]

In neo-discipleship groups there is absolute submission to the shepherd. Everyone is submitted in a regimented (army type) authoritarian chain of command. . . .

In an earlier work, Buess had warned, "Some pastors and elders set themselves up as little 'Hitlers' over the flock. . . . Some even go so far as to demand submission to themselves rather than to the Lord. . . . You cannot make a decision for yourself."[13]

Pat Robertson wrote an Open Letter to Bob Mumford on June 27, 1975, in which he complained about abuses associated with the discipleship-shepherd-submission teaching. He mentioned individuals who submit to shepherds instead of becoming responsible church members. He mentioned those who have little to say about Jesus but much about their relationship and submission to their shepherd. He told of a secretary at the Christian Broadcasting Network who had been turned into an emotional cripple by this movement. He said that she scarcely could type a letter without a long distance call to her shepherd. Robertson went on to tell about wealthy Christians being forced by their shepherds to reveal confidential details of their financial and family life. He told of one individual who was warned that he would miss out on the Kingdom of God and be ruined spiritually, physically, and financially if he did not submit to the shepherd's authority. Finally,

Robertson quoted a key figure in the shepherding movement who said that if God spoke to him and he knew that it was God speaking, but his shepherd told him to do the opposite, he would obey his shepherd.[14]

The Shepherds of Fort Lauderdale met in Oklahoma City in March of 1976 and issued the following "Statement of Concern and Regret."

> We realize that controversies and problems have arisen among Christians in various areas as a result of our teaching in relation to subjects such as submission, authority, discipling, shepherding. We deeply regret these problems and, insofar as they are due to fault on our part, we ask forgiveness from our fellow believers whom we have offended. We realize that our teachings, though we believe them to be essentially sound, have in various places been misapplied or handled in an immature way; and that this has caused problems for our brothers in the ministry. We deeply regret this and ask for forgiveness. Insofar as it lies in our power, we will do our best to correct these situations and to restore any broken relationships.
>
> (The statement is signed by Don Basham, Ern Baxter, Bob Mumford, John Poole, Derek Prince, and Charles Simpson.)[15]

Over the years since this statement, the men who were the Fort Lauderdale Shepherds have attempted to distance themselves from the negative image the shepherding movement acquired. Charles Simpson might be the one who is still most involved with covenanted leadership relationships. Even Simpson, however, has made strong efforts to clarify his former situation as a leader and advocate of shepherding. In a recent book he said,

> When the biblical qualifications for making disciples are ignored, bad things can happen. The Jim Joneses of history, the introverted cultic groups, the groups that produce serious perversions of the faith are not the re-

> sults of true spiritual authority but of perverted authority. The qualifications for making disciples and the proper kind of accountability in the ongoing leadership of God's people are necessary to healthy discipleship. In 1985, I published a public apology through *New Wine* magazine because I felt that my teachings had been misused on some occasions. I felt I had not sufficiently guarded the truths of authority and that abuses had occurred. Disciple-making without accountability and a corporate mentality should be considered intolerable in the church for biblical and historical reasons.[16]

Then Simpson added this important warning,

> The discipling relationship is not static. Hopefully, both the leader and the disciple are growing and maturing. Any possessiveness by the leader stifles this process. As I have said, it is easy for the leader to become possessive of a disciple. He may even use the phrase, "My disciple." The terminology may have a biblical basis, but it is loaded with poor connotations. A disciple belongs to the Lord. A leader only serves as a steward to help a disciple grow and mature in the Lord.[17]

The discipleship/shepherding movement has surfaced in other forms, as well. In a *Christianity Today* article, Edward E. Plowman said,

> One of the most colorful and effective Jesus-movement groups was the Christian World Liberation Front (CWLF). It was founded by Jack Sparks and a handful of fellow Campus Crusade for Christ staffers as a Crusade front in Berkeley in 1969. . . . Two months ago CWLF suffered a serious rupture. . . . Sparks was also allied with other former Campus Crusade staffers who head shepherd-disciple type ministries with a heavy emphasis on authority. A clash occurred among Sparks' house group in August on questions of authority. . . . The former Crusade staffers with whom

> Sparks is now "mutually committed" in an "apostolic band" . . . see themselves as apostles or missionaries called to set up and oversee small church groups patterned after biblical discipleship. . . . A chain of command already exists between the groups and the apostle-missionaries. This has already led to the same kind of criticism as that leveled against Bob Mumford, Derek Prince, and others in the charismatic-oriented Christian Growth Ministries of Fort Lauderdale, Florida.[18]

Strangely, the heirs of the parachurch organization known as "Campus Crusade" and the charismatic shepherding movement out of Fort Lauderdale, Florida, are thus seen to be using the same system of authoritarianism and, consequently, receiving the same kind of criticisms. The CWLF has since gone through other name changes and has finally affiliated with the Syrian Orthodox Church.

The charismatic shepherding movement moved into Roman Catholic circles just about the time of Vatican II, when Pope John XXIII was attempting to bring Roman Catholicism more into line with modern times. One of the first places where this happened was at Duquesne University in January of 1967. Some of the Catholic charismatics from Duquesne met Don Basham and Derek Prince during the peak of the shepherding enthusiasm. Roman Catholics soon began applying shepherding principles at some "intentional communities," "Christian covenant communities"—a kind of Christian commune. Those involved in this Roman Catholic application of shepherding principles published a magazine called *New Covenant*. This magazine contained articles from the Fort Lauderdale Shepherds' magazine, *New Wine*.

By 1978, five ecumenical communities had entered into covenant relationship with each other as an outgrowth of this Roman Catholic-charismatic-shepherding movement. These five communities were "Work of Christ" in East Lansing, Michigan; "Word of God" in Ann Arbor, Michigan; "People of Praise," in South Bend, Indiana; "Servants of the Light" in Minneapolis, Minnesota; and "Lamb of God" in Timonium, Maryland. James Hitchcock studied the Roman Catholic charismatic movement and found the same kind of authoritarian abuses discussed earlier in the shepherding movement—abuses very similar to those now found in the Boston Church of Christ.[19] Bruce Barron also studied the excesses of these covenant communities. What he described sounds similar to the excesses reported by those who have escaped from the Boston network of churches.[20]

Margaret Paloma wrote about the situation among Roman Catholic charismatics in her book *The Charismatic Movement*. She explained,

> Discipleship refers to the practice of making oneself personally responsible and accountable to another believer for all "life decisions." Such decisions may range from figuring a daily time schedule or financial budget to appropriate use of possessions. . . . The practice of discipleship has been advanced by a number of charismatic leaders (including Mumford 1973; Ortiz 1975). It is practiced in varying degrees in some churches as well as in many intentional communities. . . . Supporters and critics of the practice can be found among Protestant as well as Catholic charismatics.[21]

Every characteristic of discipling churches that sets them apart from other churches of Christ can be traced, directly or indirectly, to one or more of these influences discussed above. Others who have tried this approach, however, have rejected it. In a recent conversation with a leader of Maranatha Ministries, I was told, "What you are experiencing in the Church of Christ is what the charismatic movement vomited up." Maranatha Ministries is a campus movement built along the lines of the shepherding movement. They are militant in evangelism, charismatic, and authoritarian in the personal lives of their members. Their growth may exceed that of any similar movement—even that of the Crossroads/Boston churches. It may be more than an interesting coincidence that the headquarters of Maranatha Ministries is in Gainesville, Florida, not far from the Crossroads Church of Christ where the discipling movement was first introduced to churches of Christ.

In a recent conversation with a leader of Maranatha Ministries, I was told, "What you are experiencing in the Church of Christ is what the charismatic movement vomited up."

Influence on Churches of Christ

It would go beyond the purpose of this chapter and the information of this writer to trace out the full history of how the various elements of the discipling approach came into the Crossroads/Boston movement. That history can best be recorded when someone from the inner circle of founders wants to tell the story. The general outline of this story, however, is already obvious. It started with a desire to see the gospel make a greater impact on the university campus. In the late 1960s, a campus ministry organization among churches of Christ—a group known as "Campus Evangelism"—tried to learn and adapt some of the techniques Bill Bright developed in Campus Crusade. Jim Bevis, one of the Campus Evangelism leaders, went to California to train with Campus Crusade. Chuck Lucas was actively involved in the activities of Campus Evangelism at that time. It appears that some of the techniques he later introduced at Crossroads came directly from Campus Crusade. The chain, therefore, went from Campus

Crusade to Campus Evangelism to Crossroads to Boston.

In the late 1960s and early 1970s, it seemed that what was working in campus ministry was an authoritarian approach. The scene on secular university campuses was one of anarchy, rebellion, lawlessness, and rejection of all authority. What seemed to be the answer was to face the times with frontal attacks using crusades, blitzes, and militancy. This kind of environment led Campus Evangelism and its successor, Campus Advance, to adopt an aggressive "total commitment" stance. Some who were quite close to the Gainesville work could find no real fault with the approach Chuck Lucas used until well into the 1970s. At that time, the Crossroads congregation was making many converts on the University of Florida campus and looking for better ways to keep these new converts faithful. It was at that very time that the Fort Lauderdale Shepherds, Juan Carlos Ortiz, and Watchman Nee seem to have influenced the Crossroads work. It was at that same time that some connected earlier with Campus Crusade (Jack Sparks, Peter Gillquist, Jon Braun, etc.) were breaking away into their own brand of authoritarian shepherding. Some or all of these influences were probably having an impact on the Gainesville work. As time passes, however, someone formerly within this movement may tell all of this story with far more detail than can now be provided by an outside observer.

What about discipleship? If that term is used to mean being a disciple of the Lord Jesus Christ and recognizing that He has all authority, then the term is proper as one of many terms that describe the Christian life. If that term is used to mean the kind of authoritarian discipleship/shepherding movement that ran its course in various denominations in the 1960s and 1970s, then Carl Wilson's advice is appropriate. In 1976, this Pentecostal author warned that certain leaders claim authority that puts them between Christ and the people. He said that these leaders take control of the personal lives of their members by giving all sorts of orders with no biblical support at all. He concluded, "If the people of the churches concede to the clergy the right to make decisions of life and doctrine apart from the clear teaching of scripture, it will inflict the deathblow to disciple building in the churches, even as it did in the early church."[21]

Churches of Christ need to learn from what other religious groups have already experienced. They tried the discipling approach and rejected it. Churches of Christ should also reject this approach. It's time we called disciples Christians again.

Churches of Christ need to learn from what other religious groups have already experienced. They tried the discipling approach and rejected it. Churches of Christ should also reject this approach.

NOTES FOR CHAPTER 8

[1]Charles Hugo Doyle, *Guidance in Spiritual Direction* (Westminster, Maryland: The Newman Press, 1959).

[2]Dale W. Brown, *Understanding Pietism* (Grand Rapids, Michigan: Eerdmans Publishing Company, 1978). See also: F. Ernest Stoeffler, "Pietism," in *The Encyclopedia of Religion*, Volume II (New York: MacMillian, 1987), pp. 324-326.

[3]Russell T. Hitt, "Top Religious Stories Mark '75 as Pivotal Year," *Eternity*, January, 1976, p. 9.

[4]Bob Buess, *The Pendulum Swings* (Van, Texas; Sweeter Than Honey, 1974) pp. 11-13.

[5]Jerram Barrs, *Shepherds and Sheep: A Biblical View of Leading and Following* (Downers Grove, Illinois: InterVarsity Press, 1983), pp. 39-57.

[6]Betty Lee Skinner, *Daws* (Colorado Springs, Colorado: Navpress, 1986). See also: Robert D. Foster, *The Navigator* (Colorado Springs, Colorado: Navpress, 1983).

[7]Gordon MacDonald, "Disciple Abuse," *Discipleship Journal*, November 1, 1985, pp. 24-28.

[8]Richard Quebedeaux, *I Found It* (New York: Harper & Row, 1977), p. 176 ff.

[9]Edward E. Plowman, "The Deepening Rift in the Charismatic Movement," *Christianity Today*, October 10, 1975, pp. 65-66.

[10]Juan Carlos Ortiz with Jamie Buckingman, *Call to Discipleship* (Plainfield, New Jersey: Logos International, 1975).

[11]Hitt, pp. 8-9.

[12]Bob Buess, *Discipleship Pro and Con* (Van, Texas: Sweeter Than Honey, 1974), pp. 18, 48, 143.

[13]Buess, 1974, pp. 11-13.

[14]Kilian McDowell, editor, *Presence, Power, and Praise: Documents on the Charismatic Renewal*, Volume 2 (Collegeville, Minnesota: The Liturgical Press, 1980), pp. 123-126.

[15]*Ibid*. For personal reasons, John Poole removed himself from the Ft. Lauderdale Shepherds, leaving their number at five. Poole generally is not even cited with the others.

[16]Charles Simpson, *The Challenge to Care* (Ann Arbor, Michigan: Servant Publications, Vine Books, 1986), p. 101.

[17]Simpson, p. 115.

[18]Edward E. Plowman, "Whatever Happened to the Jesus Movement?" *Christianity Today*, October 24, 1975, pp. 46-48.

[19]James Hitchcock, *The New Enthusiasts and What They Are Doing to the Catholic Church* (Chicago, Illinois: Thomas Moore Press, 1982), p. 127.

[20]Bruce Barron, *If You Really Want to Follow Jesus* (Kentmore, New York: Partners Press, 1981).

[21]Margaret Paloma, *The Charismatic Movement* (Boston: Twanyne Publishers, 1982), pp. 235-236.

[22]Carl Wilson, *With Christ in the School of Disciple Building* (Grand Rapids, Michigan: Zondervan, 1976), pp. 23-24.

CHAPTER

9

WHAT OTHER RELIGIOUS GROUPS HAVE LEARNED ABOUT THE DISCIPLING MOVEMENT

What have religious leaders found objectionable and/or dangerous about the discipling movement? In this chapter, a number of observers will be quoted as they voice their concerns or their warnings about this movement which has transcended denominational barriers. The material is arranged generally in chronological order to demonstrate that the criticism has been expressed over several years and that the objections have been consistent throughout this period.

Early Warnings: The 1970s

Warnings against the abuses of authoritarian discipling appear as early as 1974. In 1974, Bob Buess wrote *The Pendulum Swings* which included warnings about the authoritarianism advocated by Watchman Nee.[1] The following year, Buess wrote *Discipleship Pro and Con* which warned about the influence of Juan Carlos Ortiz and what Buess called "neo-discipleship legalism."[2] It was on June 27, 1975, that Pat Robertson published his Open Letter to Bob Mumford listing his objections to the approach of the Fort Lauderdale Shepherds as discussed in the previous chapter. In November of that year, Mumford replied in a "Circular Letter" which explained his views on such matters as authority, shepherding, discipleship, submission, Scripture, and finances. Pat Robertson's Open Letter to Bob Mumford and Mumford's reply can be found in Volume II of *Presence, Power, and Praise: Documents on the Charismatic Renewal.*[3]

In September of 1975, Kathryn Kuhlman expressed her concern about this movement in a speech at Youngstown, Ohio. In this speech she said,

> There's a new doctrine called "the discipleship and submission movement. . . ." You may have never heard of it before. But it is so subtle and doing so much harm that if somebody doesn't do something to rebuke Satan and stop this movement, it is going to absolutely destroy the great charismatic movement. . . . Not only do they tell you to give your money to the shepherd, but to become involved in cell groups and to "reveal your deepest thoughts." I'll tell you one thing. I'm not going to tell anybody my inner thoughts.[4]

On October 10, 1975, *Christianity Today* published an article on "The Deepening Rift in the Charismatic Movement."[5] The problem discussed in this article was the same discussed by Kathryn Kuhlman in her speech at Youngstown, Ohio. Both focused on authoritarian abuses by the Fort Lauderdale Shepherds.

The Fort Lauderdale Shepherds issued a "Statement of Concern and Regret" in March of 1976 at a meeting in Oklahoma City—a statement quoted in the previous chapter. This statement, however, did not put matters to rest. Warnings continued about the difficulties, doctrinal questions, and possible emotional problems connected with the discipleship/shepherding matter. It was in 1976 that Carl Wilson published his warnings against authoritarianism in his book, *With Christ in the School of Disciple Building.*[6]

While the idea of shepherding/discipleship was running rampant throughout the loosely-structured charismatic movement, the older Pentecostal bodies such as the Assemblies of God and the Pentecostal Holiness Church already had their lines of organization. The General Presbytery of the Assemblies of God adopted a position paper on August 17, 1976, in which they took a firm stand against this movement. In this position paper, later published in tract form, the General Presbytery said,

> It is true that many new converts look to someone to keep them from error and to guide them into truth. However, where the individual relies altogether on another person to protect him from all error, he will cease searching the Scriptures and fail to develop his own ability to withstand false teaching. . . . Some find the pattern for their new order of discipleship in the relationship of Jesus with His disciples, forgetting that this was done within Judaism before Jesus began to build His Church. Instead they should seek guidance for church patterns in the Acts and Epistles. . . . Along with this there is a current tendency to downgrade democracy in the church in favor of submission to authority. . . . Jesus must be kept central. He is the great Shepherd of the sheep. The only covenant we need is the one sealed in His blood.[7]

Earlier in 1976, in the April issue of *Eternity,* Russell T. Hitt discussed this controversy in an article entitled "The Soul Watchers." In this article he reported that "in one congregation an upper middle-class family found themselves in conflict in their church because they bought a house that was not approved by their elder or 'shepherd.'" He stated that ". . . segments of both Roman Catholic and Protestant charismatic communities have been rocked by controversy over what has been labeled the 'shepherding' issue." He quoted the leader of a Roman Catholic charismatic commune who said, "Life in this community includes strict rules of submission on the part of the members who are subject to the consensus decisions of the leadership and the specific orders of the individual to whom one is submitted."

He went on to comment on the authoritarianism in Campus Crusade, the Navigators, and Robert Coleman's book *The Master Plan of Evangelism.* He then presented a key objection to this kind of authoritarianism. He said, "One of the marks of the new life in Christ is freedom. Each person, though linked organically with the body, has the privilege of individual growth. . . . To dominate a redeemed person is demeaning to him even in a human sense. In the new humanity it is even more questionable."[8]

To dominate a redeemed person is demeaning to him even in a human sense. In the new humanity it is even more questionable."[8]

By the next year, 1977, Michael Harper, leader of a prestigious British charismatic organization, was sounding his concern in the book *Let My People Grow.* In this book he made several arguments that are especially relevant for the present study.

> In more recent times some charismatics have been giving even more emphasis to what they call "discipling." But what is important to notice is that the New Testament carefully avoids using this kind of language to describe relationships between believers. Instead it uses the language of service. . . . If the language of "discipling" is used in place of "serving," it will simply be a way of replacing anarchy with tyranny. . . . One method which has been widely advocated is that adopted by Juan Carlos Ortiz in Argentina. . . . Ortiz gets his mandate for using the term "discipling" from Matthew 28:19-20. . . . It seems a strange way to inter-

> pret this command to say that Jesus tells us to make disciples for ourselves. The master-disciple relationship is, of course, used frequently to describe the relationship that Jesus had with others on earth, and, therefore, can equally describe our relationship to the Lord today. . . . But it is never in the New Testament used to describe the relationship which Christians have with one another. . . . It is best not to use the "discipling" terminology at all. Not only is it biblically unsound, but it also injects into this area an authority factor which is inappropriate.[9]

Bill Hamon's church history, *The Eternal Church,* was written from a charismatic vantage point. In this book, Hamon discusses the decade of the 1970s. One of the issues he cites is that of the discipleship, shepherding controversy. Concerning this movement, he said, "Some taught and developed a Christian leadership pyramid, chain-of-command. The pastor became almost a papal leader to those under him." He went on to observe, "All decisions had to be made by leadership, even daily and personal activities of members." Then he notes that "some disbanded the weekly united meeting of a large congregation, breaking it up into small house meeting cell groups only." Hamon concludes, however, that before the end of the 1970s, "most non-denominational Present-truth Charismatic churches had developed a balance in doctrine and practice concerning *discipleship, shepherding, family life,* and *Church structure.*"[10]

The difficulties being encountered and the subsequent criticisms, however, were by no means confined to those in the charismatic movement. In 1978, Bailey E. Smith, former president of the Southern Baptist Convention, penned his disenchantment with the discipling movement in his book *Real Evangelism.* He wrote, "When one allows someone to shadow his life as his 'spiritual leader' and dominate his thinking, he takes on the quirks, oddities and idiosyncrasies of his discipler. He becomes a disciple alright—of Tom, Henry, Bill, or Harold, but not of Jesus." He went on to tell about one leader who had produced hundreds of disciples—but every one of them had his obvious theological error. He concluded, "Their God-given distinctiveness has been absorbed by their hovering discipler."[11]

"When one allows someone to shadow his life as his 'spiritual leader' and dominate his thinking, he takes on the quirks, oddities and idiosyncrasies of his discipler. He becomes a disciple alright—of Tom, Henry, Bill, or Harold, but not of Jesus."

In 1979, Michael Green dealt with the discipleship/shepherding issue in a book on evangelism, *First Things Last: Whatever Happened to Evangelism?* In his balanced comments that recognized both strengths and weaknesses in the movement, he wrote,

> In recent years one of the fastest growing Christian organizations has been the network of house churches throughout the world. . . . Part of the strength of this movement has been the practical caring which members show for one another, not only in the practical affairs of life, but in spiritual growth and development. But so strong has been this emphasis on individual caring and what is called "delegated authority" (held in a chain going up through the pastor to the Lord) that something dangerously akin to authoritarianism can—and sometimes does—ensue. . . . Part of the value of being a Body, part of the value of a shared eldership (as you always find in the New Testament) is to preserve Christians from the vagaries of one individual leader. We need variety in those over us in the Lord.[12]

In April of 1979, David Breese wrote in *Moody Monthly* to answer the question, "Why Jonestown?" These words were written in the wake of the shock of Jim Jones having led nearly one thousand people to their death:

> It was the deadliest communion service in history. One by one—children, adults, the elderly—they took the deadly potion. Four hours later, 913 lay dead in the commune at Jonestown, Guyana. . . . The people at Jonestown were seeking an authority figure, someone who would do their thinking for them and to whom they could surrender their wills. . . . Only Jesus Christ deserves disciples. Strong leaders, clever speakers, commanding personalities—all can easily become mediators of our faith. Even many "discipleship" programs are suspiciously cultic. Jesus Christ is the only one who has earned the right to be the object of our faith.[13]

Later in 1979, David L. Waterman wrote an article on "The Care and Feeding of Growing Christians" which was published in the September issue of *Eternity*. In this article he warned,

> Christians seem to be sprouting some new terms—phrases like "personal headship," "one-on-one," "the multiplication process," "discipling relationships," "spiritual parenting," and even "spiritual pediatrics." What's going on? Afoot in many different evangelical groups, irrespective of their different brand-names, is a quiet, but persistently growing revolution in interpersonal relationships called "discipleship." You are either a "discipler" or a "disciplee," depending on your "age" and maturity in Christ and where you stand in relationship to someone else.[14]

Then Waterman quotes Chuck Miller who said,

> Discipleship is not "running people through a machine and producing Xerox copies." Too many people have seen discipling as putting people on a conveyor belt of godliness, and after so many weeks or months or years, having them go off the conveyor belt at the far end with a big "D" stamped on their foreheads meaning "discipled." Those who come off the conveyor belt seem so identical. This certainly disagrees with Scripture.[15]

He then concluded with this explanation,

> Where does all this talk about "spiritual" parenthood and reproduction come from anyway? Well, you can credit the late Dawson E. Trotman, founder of the Navigators, for most of it, at least in our generation. . . . What most people mean by discipleship today is nothing more than the post-war concept of "follow-up" in new wineskins.[16]

In October of 1979, Ronald M. Enroth, a sociologist, wrote in *Eternity* about "The Power Abusers." In this article he talked about the dependency needs of many people in our rapidly changing and often confusing world. Such people, he said, are attracted to authoritarian movements." He then charged, "The leaders of many of these groups consciously foster an unhealthy form of dependency, spiritually and otherwise, focusing on themes of submission and obedience to those in authority." He then observed,

> The so-called shepherding movement exemplifies how well-intentioned Christian leaders can bring disunity to the body of Christ and unanticipated bondage to the individual believers. It is a demonstration of how a perfectly biblical concept like authority can go awry. . . . The religious autocrat takes pleasure in requiring obedience and subordination. His style of leadership can be described as narcissistic. His message is so intertwined with his own personality (and his fear of being

> weak) that he easily concludes that anyone who disagrees with him—who is not loyal to him—is in consort with the Adversary.[17]

The Warnings Continue: The 1980s

In 1980, George Bryson wrote a booklet entitled, "Excuse for Abuse: An Examination of Heavy-Handed Authority Doctrines." This booklet begins by quoting one of the modern authoritarians who said, "What you need are people who will stand on their heads and spit nickels, merely because you tell them to, and never ask why." He then goes on to discuss some of the issues involved,

> Today, submission can mean the unqualified yielding to the one(s) in authority over you. In submission, as well as in shepherding, discipleship, and covering, right and wrong are apparently no longer determined by the merits of the act. That is, the intrinsic rightness or wrongness of an act (so judged in the light of God's Word) is not of primary concern to those holding this view. Rather, obedience to the one in authority, regardless of the request or consideration, is of prime importance. . . . Under this false definition of "authority," right is determined solely by obedience or submission to that authority or its representative. It is also contended that if the authority misdirects its "subjects," the authority will be held accountable and not the subject who obeys, even if and when the act is obviously (from a biblical standard) wrong. . . . The notion that we're responsible only to our "superiors" (and thereby absolved from responsibility to God) and that they will somehow have to answer to God for us, is totally foreign to Scripture.[18]

The false position which Bryson is refuting has a similar sound to the defense for the Nazi leaders at the Nuremburg Trials just after World War II. Even human courts of law will not allow one to be considered innocent when wrongdoing is practiced "just because someone happens to say so."

In 1981, George Mallone continued these warnings in his book *Furnace of Renewal.* He noted that,

> In the last few years, both charismatic and evangelical churches have been split over the "shepherding controversy." In its extreme, it is extortion and domination of the worst variety. . . . The movement has created alarm by its failure to understand the potentail sinfulness of leadership within the church. It is only one small step from "pastoral leadership to spiritual domination" and from "biblical submission to communitarian subservience." What is true of Lord Acton's phrase in politics is also true in religion. "All power tends to corrupt and absolute power corrupts absolutely." . . . Contrary to what we would like to believe, elders, pastors and deacons are not in a chain of command, a hierarchical pyramid, which puts them under Christ and over the church. The leaders of a biblical church are simply members of the body of Christ.[19]

That same year, 1981, Steve Coleman published a tract entitled "Christian, Who Is Your Covering?" Earlier, Coleman had lived in a "submitted house" in Austin, Texas. In the tract, he deals with the theology of "covering." He denies that obeying one's covering will offer atonement for sins which one might commit. He argues that only the blood of Christ is able to propitiate and atone. This comes to the believer through faith, not through obeying your covering. Coleman states,

> It should be apparent why the Shepherding Movement is in such error: it has applied to men what rightfully belongs to God. Instead of saying the Lord is the covering, it claims that shepherds are the covering. When the Bible says people can trust God for strength and guidance, the Shepherding Movement says that a man is necessary too. In short, the Shepherding Movement casts doubt on God's ability to care for the Christian.[20]

During 1983 and 1984, Ralph Mahoney, who edits *World Map Digest*, published a series of five articles on "The Use and the Abuse of Authority." Mahoney describes himself as "charismatic, pentecostal, and fundamental in orientation." In his first article he states,

> I carry grave concerns about the impact some charismatic teachers' concepts have on their "disciples." . . . Teaching on submission has been developed by both Protestant and Catholic groups which go far beyond the scriptural concept of submission taught in the New Testament. . . . God's Soverign Authority, the Scriptures' Veracious Authority, and the Authority of our Conscience are higher than any man, regardless of his office or title. No one on the face of the earth has a God-given right to command you to disobey your conscience, your Bible or your God. These are all above any human office or authority—be it Church, state, or otherwise.[21]

In Mahoney's fifth and last article, he gives nine examples from the Bible of those who disobeyed, with proper and good reason, someone who had "authority" over them.

In 1984, M. Thomas Starkes, a Southern Baptist writer, dealt with the new cult of neo-authoritarianism in his book *Confronting Cults: Old and New.* Starkes discussed this new cult against the backdrop of the Book of Galatians. He observed that,

> In the 1980s a new "cult" has arisen within mainline Christianity which expresses itself in various forms but may best be called "Neo-Authoritarianism." This new "cult" is of no less importance than it was in the days of Paul's letter to the Galatians in which he wrote: "Freedom is what we have—Christ has set us free! Stand, then, as free men, and do not allow yourselves to become slaves again. . . ." In his day, the legalists were Jewish men who promoted circumcision of the

> flesh as a way to please God. In the 1980s, the new legalists promote submission of the human spirit in the name of Christian discipleship. The issue is not dead. Galatians still stands as a flagship surrounded by an enemy armada seeking to rob believers of freedom in Christ Jesus.[22]

In 1982, Joyce Thurman wrote *New Wineskins: A Study of the House Church.* She did research under the guidance of Professor Walter J. Hollenweger of the University of Birmingham, England. Her master's thesis is on the house church movement in Great Britain. Those of whom she writes are charismatic, and they have had contact with the Fort Lauderdale Shepherds at the time when these leaders still advocated the full program of thoroughgoing discipleship. Interestingly, the house churches of which Thurman writes see themselves as nondenominational and sometimes use the term "Restoration Movement" to describe themselves. One chain of churches within these house churches are called "Harvestime" churches. She reports that in these churches, young couples have to seek the permission of the Elders before they become engaged. She comments that "one very dangerous area seems to be the threat to individuality, which is seen in the Harvestime Churches. Every personal wish has to be submitted before the Elders for approval before it can be acted upon."[23]

Another British writer, David Watson, was a charismatic leader and an advocate of discipleship, but he wrote words of caution in 1982. He said,

> I have seen Christians who once were relaxed and radiant, looking cowed, anxious, and fearful again, because they have come into the bondage of strict human shepherding. . . . If you show signs of thinking for yourself or personal initiative, there will be a major confrontation. Only as you conform will the fragile security of your submissive relationships with other

> Christians remain intact. . . . Dominant shepherding inevitably becomes divisive. . . . Unfortunate emphasis on shepherding, discipling and submission have been the cause of sharp controversy within the charismatic renewal (in particular) in different parts of the world.[24]

If you show signs of thinking for yourself or personal initiative, there will be a major confrontation. Only as you conform will the fragile security of your submissive relationships with other Christians remain intact. . . .

A. Boyd Luter, Jr. has written extensively on discipleship. In 1982, he wrote "A Theological Evaluation of 'Christ Model' Disciple-Making." In it he observed,

> . . . discipleship devotees reason that the presupposed "Christ and the Twelve" model is valid. . . . In scanning the works on discipling that I could find which employ the Gospels as their Scriptural base, I was struck by the "cafeteria" approach they utilized. They "pick and choose" certain practices of Jesus and the Twelve as directly applicable for discipling today, but completely overlook others according to their "taste." For example, if "doing it the way Jesus did" is really their model, why aren't they still worshipping on Saturday or offering ritual sacrifices? Why aren't they still leaving their jobs and families to physically "follow" their "discipler" as the Twelve did? Or, if they take their Gospels model seriously, why aren't they investing the same amount of time in the discipling process that Jesus and the Twelve did? In that regard, Leory Eims has estimated that Jesus spent some 13,000 hours with the Twelve. He goes on to say that even in deeply committed discipleship programs today it would take roughly 36 years to log that much time. Do you know any discipleship groups that are "playing fair" with

> these figures and these practices? . . . If Jesus Christ is to be the classic model for the "discipler," the human discipler is even doomed to mediocrity in comparison to Christ. . . . But if we attempt to employ the Gospels model, we will almost completely miss the overwhelming topic which fills Acts and the Epistles. . . . The major point here is that, if the Gospels model is adhered to, there is no obvious need for the church in the discipling process. I have even heard individuals involved in the discipleship movement say, "Why should I be involved in institutional religion? Jesus wasn't. I'm just following His example by being in a small-group discipling situation." . . . However, that attitude is exactly the opposite of the apostolic example seen in Acts. When discipling was taking place, it is clear that it was always in the context of a local church or church planting (e.g. Acts 14:21-23). . . . It is my sincere hope that the clarification attempted by this critique and alternative model will result in the further building up of Christ's church (Matt. 16:18). This will happen, however, only if the post-resurrection model is applied with the same energy and zeal as the faulty yet prevelant "Christ Model."[25]

What finally becomes of people trampled and mangled by a juggernaut approach to evangelism, discipleship, and church growth? What becomes of people who are abused in authoritarian groups? It is not too early for Christian counselors to begin preparing for those wounded by authoritarianism. Gene Edwards appears to have such a ministry among certain ones hurt by authoritarianism. His book *Letters to a Devastated Christian* would be useful for anyone who wishes to know the bitter fruits of authoritarianism. Edwards writes his book in the format of a series of letters to a young man. In the third letter, Edwards deals with the question, "Could you assess the result of the damage that has come out of the present authoritarian movement?" Edwards answers this question with eight impressions.

—Young men and young women learned how to rebuke and criticize one another when they were in an authoritarian movement. This is something no one should learn well. Sometimes rebuke gets to be an almost savage thing. Christians, especially young ones, ought not to do such things to one another.
—Pride in people's hearts was appealed to, cultivated, watered, and fertilized.
—Men and women who left those movements lost all hope in even the theoretical honesty of Christian workers. That is doubly tragic. If you lose trust in Christians, you have absolutely nowhere to go.
—Families divided—splits, separations, divorces.
—Christians lost—or never got a chance to lay hold of—the wondrous, unshackling experience of *liberty in Christ.*
—Fear and confusion became the order of the day.
—Young men and young women who might have grown up—and grown old—serving the Lord as workers were ruined . . . forever.
—Across our land have grown up little pockets of Christians who are bitter and shipwrecked. They seem to be able to find one another, move near one another, and fraternize together—like glazed-eyed beings in Dante's Inferno—forever dining on nightmares, partaking of mutual cynicism and hopelessness. *That* is the saddest of all scenes. . . . There appears to be an almost total disregard—by the leaders in these groups—of the mounting and appalling destruction resulting from authoritarianism.[26]

There appears to be an almost total disregard—by the leaders in these groups—of the mounting and appalling destruction resulting from authoritarianism.[26]

Churches of Christ cannot be blind to the bitter fruit everywhere visible from authoritarianism. Impressive numerical results must not close our eyes to the heavy toll paid by other groups which have employed these authoritarian methods. We must open our eyes to these lessons from the past. As Santayana put it, "Those who disregard the past are bound to repeat it."

NOTES FOR CHAPTER 9

[1]Bob Buess, *The Pendulum Swings* (Van, Texas: Sweeter Than Honey, 1974), pp. 11-13.
[2]Bob Buess, *Discipleship Pro and Con* (Van, Texas: Sweeter Than Honey, 1975), p. 143.
[3]Kilian McDowell (editor), *Presence, Power, Praise: Documents on the Charismatic Renewal, Volume II* (Collegeville, Minnesota: The Liturgical Press, 1980), pp. 116-147.
[4]Jamie Buckingham, *Daughter of Destiny* (Plainfield, New Jersey: Logos, 1976), pp. 286-287.
[5]Edward E. Plowman, "The Deepening Rift in the Charismatic Movement," *Christianity Today*, October 10, 1975, pp. 65-66.
[6]Carl Wilson, *With Christ in the School of Disciple Building* (Grand Rapids, Michigan: Zondervan, 1976), pp. 23-24.
[7]"The Discipleship and Submission Movement"—a position paper adopted on August 17, 1976, by the General Presbytery of the Assemblies of God (Springfield, Missouri: Gospel Publishing House, 1976). Available to public in tract form, *The Discipleship and Submission Movement*, pp. 3-14.
[8]Russell T. Hitt, "The Soul Watchers," *Eternity*, April, 1976, pp. 12-15, 34, 36.
[9]Michael Harper, *Let My People Grow* (Plainfield, New Jersey: Logos, 1977), pp. 74-75, 151-153.
[10]Bill Hamon, *The Eternal Church* (Phoenix, Arizona: Christian International Publishers, 1982), pp. 286-287.
[11]Bailey E. Smith, *Real Evangelism* (Nashville, Tennessee: Broadman Press, 1978), p. 18.
[12]Michael Green, *First Things Last: Whatever Happened to Evangelism?* (Nashville, Tennessee: Discipleship Resources, 1979), pp. 57-58.
[13]Dave Breese, "Why Jonestown?" *Moody Monthly*, April, 1979, pp. 42-43.
[14]David L. Waterman, "The Care and Feeding of Growing Christians," *Eternity*, September, 1979, p. 17.
[15]*Ibid.*, p. 18.
[16]*Ibid.*, p. 19.
[17]Ronald M. Enroth, "The Power Abusers: When Follow-the-Leader Becomes a Dangerous Game," *Eternity*, October, 1979, pp. 23ff.
[18]George Bryson, "Excuse for Abuse: An Examination of Heavy-Handed Authority Doctrines," *The Word for Today, Special Edition 2*, 1980, pp. 1-7.
[19]George Mallone, *Furnace of Renewal: A Vision for the Church* (Downers Grove, Illinois: InterVarsity Press, 1981), pp. 83-85.
[20]Steve Coleman, "A Christian Look at the Shepherding Movement," *Personal Freedom Outreach*, April-June, 1983, later published as a tract, "Christian, Who Is Your Covering?"

[21]Ralph Mahoney, "The Use and Abuse of Authority Part One," *World Map Digest*, 1983-1984. November/December, 1983, pp. 7, 8, 11.

[22]M. Thomas Starkes, *Confronting Cults: Old and New* (Chattanooga, Tennessee: AMG, 1984), pp. 127ff.

[23]Joyce Thurman, *New Wineskins: A Study of the House Church* (Frankfurt: Verlag Peter Lang, 1982), pp. 99ff.

[24]David Watson, *Called and Committed: World Changing Discipleship* (Wheaton, Illinois: Harold Shaw Publishers, 1982), pp. 45ff.

[25]A. Boyd Luter, Jr., "A Theological Evaluation of 'Christ Model' Disciple-Building," 1982, *The Journal of Pastoral Practice*, pp. 11-21.

[26]Gene Edwards, *Letters to Devastated Christians* (Goleta, California: Christian Books, 1983), pp. 10-11.

A SELECT ANNOTATED BIBLIOGRAPHY OF MATERIALS GENERALLY UNFAVORABLE TO MODERN AUTHORITARIAN DISCIPLING TACTICS

prepared by Don Vinzant

Adams, Jay E. "Discipling, Counseling and Church Discipline," *The Journal of Pastoral Practice,* volume VII, no. 3 (1984).

This article is a revision of Adams' speech in 1983, to The National Association of Nouthetic Counselors. He deals with biblical and pragmatic considerations of church discipline. Discipline is imperative. It is one of the marks of the true church.

Adams' approach to counseling involves the use of confrontation. The Crossroads/Boston Movement has used his basic book on counseling as a textbook in their discipling activities.

In this article, Adams makes it plain that he is not in favor of one person dominating another nor trying to follow and become like some contemporary teacher—it is rather "becoming like Jesus Christ" (p. 19).

Alcorn, Wallace Arthur. "The Biblical Concept of Discipleship as Education for Ministry." Dissertation for Doctor of Philosophy in the School of Education, New York University, 1974.

A full-length work, 341 pages, Alcorn's dissertation draws on the Old Testament, as well as the New, for insights. He offers some interesting questions about contemporary seminary education in the light of discipleship principles extracted from Scripture.

Alcorn suggests that it might prove worthwhile to study personality types with reference to some who might have a tendency toward overdependency. Further, he questions whether some might seek discipleship for personal security. He wonders if there might be a way to predict such potential problems and initiate methods to avoid such problems. (p. 323, no. 1).

This work deserves a wider circulation.

Barron, Bruce. *If You Really Want To Follow Jesus.* Kentmore, N.Y.: Partners Press, 1981.

A hard-hitting study of "covenant community." Barron looks most closely at Work of Christ, a closely co-ordinated community, ecumenical, yet Roman Catholic in orientation, located in Lansing, Michigan.

These intentional communities make much of headship/submission doctrines. They appear to have been influenced by some of the earlier teachings of discipleship/shepherding as taught in *New Wine* and the Bob Mumford team out of Fort Lauderdale.

Barrs, Jerram. *Shepherds and Sheep: A Biblical View of Leading and Following,* Downers Grove, Ill.: InterVarsity Press, 1983.

An indispensible book for those wishing to make a detailed study of this subject. Chapter Three on "Some Danger Areas," (pp. 39-57), is much to the point in its warnings on modern authoritarianism and also the modern arrogation of the title "apostles."

Bolt, Martin and David G. Myers. *The Human Connection: How People Change People.* Downers Grove, Ill.: InterVarsity Press, 1984.

In chapter nine, (pp. 95-107), Bolt suggests some half a dozen techniques to help prevent "groupthink." Groupthink occurs when dissent is suppressed in order to enhance group harmony. Hard analysis and critical judging of pros and cons is short-circuited to sustain consensus. Bolt follows a recent study by Irving L. Janis on the victims of groupthink. The techniques to prevent groupthink are these:

1. Leader encourages every member to express doubts and articulate his objections.
2. Sub-divide large group and have different persons chair the sessions then come back and hammer out the differences.
3. Bring in outside experts to present information and challenge ideas.
4. Leaders refrain from stating their position, preference or expectations.
5. At each meeting, assign a different person to be "the devil's advocate.
6. Have a "second chance" meeting before decisions are implemented.

If Crossroads/Boston employed these techniques, their critics might be silenced.

Breese, Dave. "Why Jonestown?" *Moody Monthly*, April, 1979, pp. 42-43.

Brief, but quite thought-provoking on possible parallels which could occur to Boston unless precautions are observed.

Brown, Dale W. *Understanding Pietism*. Grand Rapids, Michigan: Eerdmans Publishing Company, 1978.

A recent book incorporating research done for a doctoral dissertation on Pietism, Brown goes back to P. J. Spener and A. H. Francke (whom he calls "churchly Pietists"), for roots of this emphasis. Brown calls Pietism "one of the least understood movements in Judeo-Christian history." He further mentions Pietism's "tremendous influence on Christian life in the United States."

A careful look at Pietism's practices and negative tendencies produces an unexpected foreshadowing of some discipling work being done today.

Bryson, George. "Excuse for Abuse: An Examination of Heavy-handed Authority Doctrines," *The Word For Today—Special Edition 2*, pp. 1-7.

Bryson states his opinion that the Scriptures do not authorize present-day apostles. He further reminds his readers that 1 Peter 5:3 teaches elders not to be lords, but rather to be examples to the flock. He says, "Far from undermining spiritual authority, this definition . . . is a much more effective and powerful force for good than the "Me boss, you brother" mentality so prevalent in many circles.

Buess, Bob. *Discipleship: Pro and Con*. Van, Texas: Sweeter Than Honey, 1975.

Buess, an East Texas charismatic pastor, is the first person I have found who sounds the alarm about the dangers in "neo-discipleship" or dictatorial submission teachings.

Calenberg, Richard D. "The New Testament Doctrine of Discipleship." Dissertation for Doctor of Theology, Grace Theological Seminary, 1981.

Looking at the New Testament evidence on the subject, Calenberg produces a 278 page dissertation which attempts to deal with exegetical fairness. Calenberg notices, at the beginning of his study, that, when the dissertation was written, 1981, "discipleship" was a "shibboleth" which all evangelicals were to utter repeatedly, but which few could define biblically.

Calenberg concludes that the term "disciple" is absent from the New Testament Epistles because of what the term would have connoted in the Greek world and because the relationship between the believer and his Lord was better communicated with terms during the Church Age. His conclusion, further, is that upon saving faith one becomes a disciple in a general sense and subsequently one makes the deeper commitment to the stringent requirements for true discipleship.

Coleman, Steve. "A Christian Look at the Shepherding Movement," *Personal Freedom Outreach*, vol. 3, no. 2. April/June, 1983.

Brief, but powerful, as Coleman finds the "covering" doctrine which tells the modern disciple to obey implicitly every teaching of his discipler to be woefully deficient theologically. The covering doctrine argues that if one's discipler gave him an erroneous command to obey—the disciple is covered if he obeys it. His implicit obedience makes his covering. The discipler is held responsible for giving a wrong command. Coleman shows how this undercuts, theologically, Christ and His sacrifice as the only thing that can atone for sin.

Davison, Roy. *Doctrinal Errors of the Hierarchical Discipleship Movement.* Belgium: privately printed booklet, 1985.

A concise booklet of 43 pages in which this veteran missionary of 20 years in Europe traces much of modern discipleship back to Robert Coleman's *The Master Plan of Evangelism* and to Juan Carolos Ortiz' *Call to Discipleship.* Davison concludes that some are in danger of being "deceived and led astray." They are, ". . . those for whom numerical 'success' is more important than truth, those who are intrigued by human theories and doctrines, those who prefer being told what to do rather than accepting their own responsibility, and those who like to exercise authority over others." (p. 40).

Deffenbaugh, Don. *The Discipling Movement Among Churches of Christ.* private tract. Neosho, Missouri, 1986.

A recent study which traces much of the influence toward modern discipleship to Robert Coleman's *The Master Plan of Evangelism.* (see chapter eight in this book on "Roots.") Deffenbaugh states that in 1980, some 200 congregations were troubled by this movement of modern discipleship. He mentions that congregations in more than 22 states have suffered division because of it. (p. 8).

In his addendum, he observes that "The discipling movement has been rather successful among the young adults in the Lord's church, especially those . . . of college age who are insecure and unsettled and are looking for direction in their lives. This system provides for them that acceptance and direction at a very crucial time. That is why the discipling movement has seemed to work so well in the college and university community." (p. 27).

Dixon, Danny Andre. *Discipling Ministries: An Inside Look,* Nashville, Tenn.: Gospel Advocate Company, 1987. 73 pp.

A recent book by one who formerly worked within the ranks of the modern discipling movement. In nine chapters and an appendix, Dixon examines some aspects of this movement and what he found to be deficient and legalistic.

Edwards, Gene. *Letters to a Devastated Christian.* Goleta, Calif.: Christian Books, 1983.

A brief book of only 39 pages. Edwards, experienced in counseling those wounded by authoritarianism, gives advice within the literary framework of letters to a young man, "Ken." One of Edwards' tests for determining if one is in an authoritarian movement is to ask how many ex-elders there are. Another is to ask if the one leading the movement has to control everyone "within his envirionment."

Another suggestion is to give out a boxful of George Orwell's book, *Animal Farm.* Give them out to all one's friends within the movement—to the leaders, elders, etc. If those in the movement can read that book and survive, Edwards says, ". . . then, I don't think you are in an authoritarian movement."

In a more serious vein, Edwards (p. 10) gives eight impressions he has developed as to the damage done by authoritarianism in shepherding/discipleship.

Enroth, Ronald M. "Churches on the Fringe," *Eternity,* October, 1986, pp. 17ff.

This article is to be followed by a book in 1988, to be published by InterVarsity Press. These churches, ". . . promote isolationist attitudes, exhibit a sense of spiritual superiority, and scrutinize members who want to leave their groups. Some former members feel victimized, confused and bitter."

Enroth concludes that mainstream churches must reach out to the ones on the fringe who feel hurt and confusion and help them find healing.

Anyone dealing in any way with authoritarianism would want to read Enroth's upcoming book.

Enroth, Ronald M. "The Power Abusers: When Follow-the-Leader Becomes A Dangerous Game," *Eternity,* October, 1979, pp. 22ff.

Connected to Enroth's article is a one-page box treatment of Covenant Presbyterian Church of Philadelphia. It was examined and several former members interviewed by the local presbytery. This presbytery found seven similarities of Covenant Presbyterian with cultic groups. Some sound strangely similar to the authoritarian movement within Crossroads/Boston. "(1) The presence of a strong leader; (2) a faithful inner group which implicitly accepts all that the leader sets forth; (3) the gathering of weaker persons between the ages of 15 and 30 and marshalling them into a monolithic fixation; (4) the destruction of liberty of conscience; (5) the accepting of biblical truths, as most cults do, and then adding to and taking from them; (6) alienating young people from their parents, since they present a competing authority figure; (7) and finally, a developing and ever sharpened expertise in techniques of brainwashing." (p. 24).

Fialka, John J. "Fervent Faction—Maranatha Christians, Backing Rightist Ideas, Draw Fire Over Tactics," *Wall Street Journal,* August 16, 1985.

Maranatha Ministries, based in Gainesville, Florida, and led by Bob Weiner, Jr., received careful scrutiny by Fialka. Critics find Maranatha using a form of mind control. Students are isolated from their parents and are guided as to their decisions by those leading the Maranatha.

One young woman who had entered the Maranatha movement at age 23, Kathy Myatt, says that when she questioned some church rulings, she was said to have "a spirit of independent thinking and rebellion."

In a telephone interview with a Maranatha spokesperson, I (DV) was told that Maranatha was just helping students who weren't reared properly and "didn't know how to brush their teeth." This spokesperson quickly and forcefully rejected however, any implication that Maranatha was like Crossroads (at one time also headquartered in Gainesville, Florida). He said of the troubles we are experiencing in Crossroads/Boston, "What you are experiencing in the Church of Christ is what the charismatics vomited up."

Green, Michael. *First Things Last: Whatever Happened to Evangelism?* Nashville, Tenn.: Discipleship Resources, 1979.

His warnings merit attention. Green is perhaps the foremost scholar on evangelism in the first century. Green is concerned that the aftercare for new Christians not become oppressive.

Griffiths, Michael. *The Example of Jesus.* Downers Grove, Ill.: InterVarsity Press, 1985.

Griffiths, principal of London Bible College, reminds his readers that, "It is striking that the apostles never refer to their own converts as being their own disciples (the word is never used, even once in any of the Epistles), but win their converts to their departed Master, baptising them in His name, and into a new community in Christ, with Christ as their head."

Gustaitis, Rasa. "Hard-Sell Religion," *Nutshell*, Fall, 1983. pp. 72ff.

An up-close critical examination of Boston-style discipleship as Gustaitis found it to be in 1983. This article also deals with the Maranatha Ministries, referred to in the article by Fialka.

Gustaitis turns in a rather grim report.

Hach, Robert (editor). "The Authority Structure of the Church," and "Spiritual Leadership: Leading or Lording?" *Reflections*, Volume 1, Number 5, October, 1987, pp. 1-4.

Anyone interested in thoughtful articles by those who know what they are talking about should request *Reflections*. Hach, and others who work with him in Miami, come to this writing assignment from a vantage point of knowledgeability about Crossroads/Boston.

Hadaway, C. Kirk, Stuart A. Wright, and Francis M. DuBose. *Home Cell Groups and House Churches*. Nashville, Tenn.: Broadman Press, 1987.

This recent Southern Baptist work gives a dispassionate and objective look at the entire small-group emphasis. As they deal with house churches, they find it necessary to report on the shepherding movement as it was led in earlier years by Mumford, Simpson, Prince, etc., out of Fort Lauderdale, Florida.

Hadfield, Ron. "Campus Advance Defectors Speak of Experiences," *The Optimist*, (student newspaper at Abilene Christian University), Volume 66, Number 26, April 13, 1979.

An indispensible source for those wanting to know what effect the Crossroads Movement was having on young people in the late '70s. This material can be ordered from Abilene Christian University.

Harper, Michael. *Let My People Grow: Ministry and Leadership in the Church*. Plainfield, New Jersey: Logos International, 1977.

Harper, former associate with John Stott, went into the charismatic movement and became the director of Fountain Trust. A respected leader, he sounds an alert to a kind of leadership in house churches which could become oppressive. His warnings are quite applicable to those in authoritarian movements in churches of Christ.

Hart, Larry. "Problems of Authority in Pentecostalism," *Review and Expositor*, vol. 75, no. 2 (Spring, 1978). pp. 249ff.

Writing from a Southern Baptist standpoint, Hart, nevertheless, deals with the problem of radical submission in the discipleship "family" to which one belonged. The movement, Hart says, in some circles, degenerated into what he calls "extreme authoritarianism and exclusivism."

One wonders how many warnings our own discipleship advocates must hear before they take heed to where their own excesses can lead.

Hendren, Bob. *Which Way The Church?* Nashville, Tenn.: 20th Century Christian, 1985.

This has been the premier book on Crossroads/Boston which this writer (DV) has found. Everyone interested in the subject should purchase the book and read it at least twice.

Hitt, Russell T. "The Soul-Watchers," *Eternity*. April, 1976, pp. 13ff.

A most useful article for the one beginning to explore the field of modern discipleship teaching.

Huang, Thomas T. "Boston Church Recruits Pursue Interphase Frosh," *The Tech* (M.I.T.), September 1, 1987, pp. 1,11.

On the campus of M.I.T., in Boston, the accusation was brought that this past summer some Boston recruiters used too much pressure in trying to influence foreign students.

A middle way of speaking the truth in love must be found—a way that would avoid indifference on the one hand and would avoid pressure and exploitation of lonely young people on the other hand.

Jennings, Alvin. "Where Do I Stand In Relation To the Crossroad Churches?" Fort Worth, Texas: Star Bible Publications, dated September 30, 1987. 4 pps.

Earlier Jennings appeared to be an admirer and friend to the Crossroads/Boston Movement. In this tract, Jennings states that he has several concerns, one of the principal ones being in the area of organization—both in local churches and in Boston's new "pillar" approach.

Jennings refers to a recent speech by Dr. Jerry Jones. Since Jones voiced some of the same concerns as Jennings, there is given a brief synopsis of Jones' speech. It covered four points: (1) Proper Use of Scripture; (2) Discipling Models; (3) Re-baptism and (4) Local Leadership.

Kachur, Robert M. "Special Report: Campus Cultic Groups," *U*, (April/May) 1987, pp. 2ff.

Kachur suggests that the typical person joining a cult or sect is between 17 and 25 and, for the first time living away from home. They come from middle-class or upper middle-class homes. They have sometimes lost someone close to them, . . . have perhaps just broken up with a sweetheart, feel that their lives lack a sense of "drama, power and vitality."

Those involved in campus evangelism need to avoid abuse, exploitation and domineering of young people. In addition to the Christian ethical considerations, those involved in campus evangelism must remember that these young people will inevitably mature and grow older and wiser. Then, when they look back on their experience, the question will be faced—do they feel they were loved or used?

Lattin, Don. "The Shepherding Movement," *San Francisco Examiner*, February 19, 1984, Section A, pp. 1ff.

An excellent article by a reporter for a secular daily newspaper on what is involved in being a part of the shepherding movement. "Those in the movement concede they regularly seek their shepherd's counsel before making major personal decisions. They willingly quit their jobs, sell their homes and move when church leaders tell them to relocate."

Those who have never been a part of these discipleship/shepherding movements may have difficulty believing the degree of dependence which is fostered within these groups, but Lattin's article states it plainly.

Ligon, Bill and Robert Paul Lamb. *Discipleship: The Jesus View*. Plainfield, N.J.: Logos International, 1979.

Ligon has done a real service in supplying one of the few historical treatments of a discipleship emphasis as it has been manifested throughout the centuries since the Church was established.

Looney, John Thomas, "Nondenominational Charismatic Churches: Visions of a New Testament Community," Thesis for Master of Divinity at Union Theological Seminary (New York), December, 1981.

Looney, who had been a part of the shepherding movement as seen in the Fort Lauderdale shepherds, wrote a master's thesis which examined the bases of this approach. His "insider" status adds interest to his treatment.

Looney left this movement and is now a pastor in the Christian and Missionary Alliance Church in New York.

Luter, A. Boyd, "A New Testament Theology of Discipling," Dissertation for Doctor of Theology, Dallas Theological Seminary, May 1985.

This massive dissertation of 245 pages brings together several concerns which Luter has treated earlier in periodical articles. Luter deals with the uniqueness of Christ's person and position as a discipler. (p. 37ff). This being the case, where does one find the warrant to presume to say that today Christians are to take the role of discipler and apply all the principles Christ used in His unique place to themselves? "Christ's example as a discipler cannot be imitated to the extent the popular model insists on." (p. 38).

He finds a major difference between what Christ was doing in the Gospels to make apostles and what leaders are to do today is that today the Church exists. It was not present during Christ's earthly ministry. It today has a major role in nurturing and developing young Christians.

Luter, A. Boyd, Jr. "A Theological Evaluation of "Christ Model" Disciple-Making," *The Journal of Pastoral Practice,* volume 5, number 4, 1982. pp. 11-21.

Luter has done a real service to the evangelical world in challenging the modern discipleship advocates to come up with some justification for their presumptuously using the "Christ Model" as their model for disciple-making. In this article and in his dissertation later, Luter shows the non-applicability of much of Christ's work in training the Twelve to our contemporary situation. The would-be discipler today has neither the position nor the place Christ held. He cannot point to his own life as sinless as Christ's followers could point to the perfection of their model. Today's discipler lacks the time, authority, and, doubtless, the humility, to arrogate the model Christ exemplified.

It is absolutely unfair as Luter points out, to pick, choose and select, without solid hermeneutical footing, among the various things Christ did and claim that you are replicating today what He did then in preparing His own apostles.

Lynch, Selma, "Forum: Letter to the Editor" *Christian Chronicle.* volume 43, no. 9, September, 1986, p. 23.

This young lady is reacting to an editoral in the April, 1986, *Chronicle.* She recounts her own experience in the Crossroads movement. She tells about a woman who came to the church, studied and wanted to be baptized. The woman counselor said she was not ready. The woman went to the preacher of the congregation. He was not a part of Crossroads. He talked to her, then baptized her. The Crossroads people were furious. They shunned her, heavily criticized her, basically excluding her from their circle of friends. The new convert left the church, confused and heart-broken. Ms. Lynch decided to leave the Crossroads approach and move to a mainline Church of Christ where she found warm, caring Christians who loved her. Before she left Crossroads, she tells of her cousin coming by to find out why she was leaving. Her cousin said, "If it bothers you to have people telling you what to do, don't worry. When you've been in the movement longer, then you can tell others what to do."

Lynch says, "Apparently it's run like a *pyramid scam.* As you're in the movement over time, you get moved into positions of greater authority and control. . . ."

MacDonald, Gordon. "Disciple Abuse," *Discipleship Journal,* A Navigators publication, volume 5, no. 6 Issue Thirty (November 1, 1985), pp. 24-28.

A very thoughtful article by one who had comprehensive knowledge of the entire evangelical world. It bears careful reading and reflection. I would rank this as among the four or five most important things to read on this problem.

It is to the credit of the Navigators who use the discipleship vocabulary extensively that in their own journal they would publish articles such as MacDonald's.

McDonnell, Kilian. (editor). *Presence, Power, Praise: Documents on the Charismatic Renewal, Volume 2*, Continental, National, and Regional Documents, Numbers 38-80, 1975-1979. Collegeville, Minnesota: The Liturgical Press, 1980. (pp. 116-147).

This three volume collection of documents having to do with the charismatic movement is of great historical value to those researching this specialized field. The section cited above is that which deals with the "first holy war" of the charismatics which had to do with shepherding/discipleship and its ancillary doctrines.

MacGavran, Donald. "How About That New Verb to Disciple?" *Growth Bulletin*, Volume XV, No. 5 (May, 1979), pp. 1ff.

The dean of the Church Growth Movement defines and explains the different ways people are using the verb "to disciple" which MacGavran coined in his earlier writings on church growth.

Mahoney, Ralph. "The Use and Abuse of Authority," *World Map Digest*, 1983/1984.

Mahoney writes as one within the charismatic movement in his strictures on authority. He has five articles dealing with the issue of authority in the setting of the problems which the charismatic movement has undergone.

In his fifth and last article, Mahoney brings forward nine examples of cases recorded within the Bible in which someone was doing the Lord's will by disobeying what someone with authority over them had told them they must do.

Miller, Elliot. "The Christian and Authority," Parts One and Two, *Forward*, Spring, 1985 and Summer, 1985.

In this two-part introductory study, Miller lays out plainly and with surprising fullness the whole question of the church and authority. He sees the issue in historical perspective. After dealing with authoritarianism in the historic church, Miller moves to authoritarianism in the contemporary church. He says that the esteemed leader, minister or shepherd often ". . . will not hesitate to pronounce God's will for the minutiae of their followers' personal lives (this is one of the areas in which the abuse and devastation surpass those in the traditionalist churches). Miller mentions that in different degrees this can be found in a whole gamut of evangelical Protestant groups. The first group he refers to is "the 'Shepherding and Discipleship' movement (which teaches the doctrine that every believer needs a fellow-believer as a 'covering')." (p. 13 in Part One).

Noll, M.A., "Pietism," *Evangelical Dictionary of Theology*, (edited by W.A. Elwell) Grand Rapids, Mich.: Baker Book House, pp. 855ff.

Noll's article is balanced and suggests both the positive and negative tendencies to be found resulting from the application of Pietistic influences. With respect to the negative results, Noll says, "Some of the fears of its earliest opponents have been partially justified. At its worst the pietistic tendency can lead to inordinate subjectivism and emotionalism; it can discourage careful scholarship; it can fragment the church through enthusiastic separatism; it can establish new codes of almost legalistic morality; and it can underrate the value of Christian tradition." (p. 858). That sounds like a criticism of the worst scenario of the moden authoritarian discipleship movement among Crossroads/Boston.

O'Malley, J. S., "Discipleship Movement," *Evangelical Dictionary of Theology,* (edited by Walter A. Elwell), Grand Rapids, Mich.: Baker Book House, 1984., pp. 319-320.

An article which is indispensible to understand shepherding/discipleship as it grew out of the charismatic movement. O'Malley points out that, "Some oppose the amount of control exercised by shepherds over such matters as the choice of a mate and the decision to have children." (p. 320)

Smith, Chuck. "Shepherding or Dictatorship? Christian Possession," *The Answer for Today,* 6, 1979, pp. 1-5.

A brief, but useful, article by one who was a prime early leader in the "Jesus People" movement of the 1960s. Smith talks about the problem, "If you want to buy or sell your house, it's imperative that you first consult your elder. . . . The same is true if you want to buy or sell a car or TV, or if you want to change your job. If you want to go on a trip, these shepherds will tell you where you can go, how long you can stay, and when to be back. . . . If you desire to move to another locality, they'll tell you whether or not you may have their blessings and permission. . . . The elders have set up an apostleship. . . . On many occasions these shepherds have told a person exactly whom he or she was to marry, how much and when to give, what books to read, and which tapes to listen to. . . . It is absolutely imperative to obey your elder—even if he is wrong. . . . What you do will be right, because you've done it in obedience to your elder." (p. 2).

It sounds to critics of Crossroads/Boston as if they are on the verge of teaching all of the above, if indeed they are not already in the middle of teaching all of the above.

Starkes, M. Thomas. *Confronting Cults: Old and New.* Chattanooga, Tenn.: AMG, 1984.

Starkes discusses many cults and cult-like groups. On the issue of authoritarianism, he has an entire chapter. He calls chapter 12, "Neo-Authoritarianism: A Psycho-Theological Struggle." Starkes says, "In the 1980's, the new legalists promote submission of the human spirit in the name of Christian discipleship. The issue is not dead. Galatians still stands as a flagship surrounded by an enemy armada seeking to rob believers of freedom in Christ Jesus." (p. 127).

Stoeffler, F. Ernest, "Pietism," *The Encylopedia of Religion,* New York: MacMillan, 1987, (edited by Mircea Eliade). Volume 11, pp. 324-326.

Stoeffler's article differentiates between various early branches of Pietism. He mentions that Pietism must now be viewed as one of the major religious traditions which shaped Protestantism in America. He states in summary fashion a number of positive contributions of Pietism.

Terris, Daniel. "Come, All Ye Faithful," *Globe Magazine,* 1986.

Rather critical of the Boston Church of Christ, Terris' article deserves to be read by both friends and foes. Terris' interviews are especially valuable and cover a wide range of feeling toward what the Crossroads/Boston movement is doing.

"The Discipleship and Submission Movement," Springfield, MO.: Gospel Publishing House, 1976. (A position paper adopted August 17, 1976, published as a tract.)

The old-line Pentecostal denominations such as The Assemblies of God and Pentecostal Holiness Church did not fall victim, by and large, to the shepherding/discipleship fad that rocked the charismatic movement in the mid-1970's.

The Assemblies of God set up a committee to study this issue and then the General Presbytery adopted their position paper and published it as a tract which can be ordered from the denominational headquarters. It takes a firm stand against the discipleship and submission movement.

Thompson, James. *The Mark of A Christian*. Broken Arrow, Okla.: Christian Communications, 1983.

In his discussions on Paul's methods and those of his opponents in 2 Corinthians 10-13, Thompson offers some judicious thoughts for leadership which are relevant to the issue at hand.

Thurman, Joyce. *New Wineskins: A Study of the House Church*. Frankfurt: Verlag Peter Lang, 1982.

A ground-breaking study of a phenomenon in Great Britain—the house church—which was not well-known here in the United States. Thurman, through reading and interviews, paints an intriguing portrait of these churches—charismatic—which use the term "Restoration Movement" to describe themselves. One of the darker aspects into which the Harvestime branch of these house churches have fallen is the use of authoritarian tactics in dealing with their members. The Harvestime leaders came in contact with the shepherding movement emanating from Fort Lauderdale, Florida.

Waterman, David L. "The Care and Feeding of Growing Christians," *Eternity*, 1979, pp. 17-22.

A valuable article giving some of the background of when "follow-up" began to be called "discipling." Waterman sees a strong influence in aftercare of new converts from Dawson Trotman, the founder of the navigators.

Wilson, Carl. *With Christ in the School of Disciple Building*. Grand Rapids, Michigan: Zondervan, 1976.

An important book which deserves to be better known. Wilson sounds an alarm against the hierarchy which he realized could doom the modern discipleship emphasis.

PART IV

A REFERENCE GUIDE TO THE DISCIPLING MOVEMENT AMONG CHURCHES OF CHRIST

by Gene Vinzant

ABOUT THE AUTHOR

Gene Vinzant was born in Sao Paulo, Brazil, while his parents, Don and Carol Vinzant, were serving as missionaries. He graduated from Oklahoma Christian College in 1984 with highest honors. While attending OCC, Gene met and married Becky Yeakley, daughter of Flavil and Maydell Yeakley.

Gene graduated from Abilene Christian University in August of 1987 with a Master of Divinity degree. While at ACU, Gene worked with Flavil Yeakley in the Church Growth Institute as a research assistant. Gene works as a full-time minister and hopes to return to Brazil as a missionary.

CHAPTER

11

A GUIDE TO THE DISCIPLING MOVEMENT

A Chronology of the Church Plantings of the Boston Movement

A great deal of the fascination with the "Boston Movement" is based on their rapid numerical growth. While Boston's growth alone is impressive, the growth achieved through Boston's church plantings is even more impressive. That growth has come mainly from direct plantings by Boston or Boston daughter churches. Additional growth has come as a result of Boston's takeover of churches which were under the influence of the Crossroads Church of Christ in Gainesville, Florida. The story of the Boston Movement's growth begins in June of 1979 and continues today. The following chronology is based primarily on information contained in the August 30, 1987, bulletin of the Boston Church of Christ.

June 1979: Boston Church of Christ

Kip McKean, and his wife Elena, moved with a small group of young people to work with the Lexington, Massachusetts, Church of Christ. The beginning of membership of the group in June was 30. The church grew rapidly, baptizing over 4,000 by the fall of 1987.

June 1982: Chicago Church of Christ

Boston planted its first daughter church in Chicago. Under the leadership of evangelist Marty Fuqua, the church baptized almost 900 people by the fall of 1987. Chicago planted a church in Minneapolis-St. Paul and "replanted" a church in St. Louis.

July 1982: Central London Church of Christ

Boston calls this church "the largest and fastest-growing congregation outside the borders of the United States." By the fall of 1987, this church had baptized over 800 people. The London church planted a church in Sydney, Australia, in 1987.

June 1983: New York City Church of Christ

Under the leadership of "lead evangelist" Steve Johnson, the New York church baptized well over 1,000 by August 1987. Boston calls this "the second fastest-growing church in all the world." A church planting was sent to São Paulo, Brazil, in the summer of 1987.

June 1985: Providence Church of Christ

Formerly a house church within the Boston congregation, Providence became a separate congregation. In their first two years they baptized 135 individuals. According to the Boston newsletter, Providence is "the prototype of how the gospel will spread from the large cities to surrounding small cities."

August 1985: Central Toronto Church of Christ

The Toronto church was planted by evangelists Mark Mancini and Henry Kriete. Having baptized 250 in the first two years and with an attendance of 320, this is "the largest and fastest growing church in all of Canada."

June 1986: Johannesburg Church of Christ

This multi-racial South African church baptized close to 100 in its first year, making it "one of the fastest-growing churches in Africa."

August 1986: Central Paris Church of Christ

Under the direction of evangelist Tom Turnbull, the

Paris church baptized 42 in its first year, becoming "the largest and fastest-growing church in French-speaking Europe." This was the first non-English speaking church planted by Boston.

October 1986: Stockholm Church of Christ

The Stockholm church baptized 40 people by August of 1987. They are "the largest and fastest-growing church in all of Scandinavia."

January 1987: Bombay Church of Christ

The Boston newsletter claims that this church is "the largest church of Christ in all India with an attendance of 100, with over 40 baptisms this year."

January 1987: Kingston Church of Christ

This Jamaican church was Boston's first "replanting." A "replanting" is Boston's term for taking over the control and supervision of an existing church. The Kingston Church baptized 80 between the replanting and August of 1987.

A "replanting" is Boston's term for taking over the control and supervision of an existing church.

January 1987: Twin Cities Church of Christ

This is the first "granddaughter" of the Boston church. The Chicago church planted and directs this work in Minneapolis-St. Paul. There have been 60 baptisms as of August, 1987.

February 1987: Sydney Church of Christ

The Central London church "replanted" this church in Sydney, Australia. A total of 85 were baptized in the first seven months of this work.

June 1987: São Paulo Church of Christ

The New York City church planted this work in São Paulo, Brazil, the largest city in South America. Twenty-one people were baptized in the first two months.

August 1987: St. Louis Church of Christ

The Chicago church "replanted" this church which was originally planted by the Shandon Church of Christ in Columbia, South Carolina. With a beginning membership of 75, 14 were baptized in the first month after the takeover.

August 1987: Atlanta Church of Christ

The July 26, 1987, bulletin of the Boston church describes the creation of this church from a "Christian remnant." This church was planted after the Atlanta Highlands Church of Christ resisted "such biblical principles as the authority of the evangelist, one-on-one discipleship and the calling of every member to evangelism." A team consisting of Andy Lindo, other evangelists, and 15 full-time interns will direct the church for one year, while Sam Laing is trained in Boston to become the "lead evangelist."

September 1987: San Francisco Church of Christ

This congregation was originally the Berkeley Church of Christ. The August 16, 1987, Boston bulletin describes the decision of the Boston church to "rebuild" and "officially direct" this church. The Boston elders and Kip McKean decided to call this operation a "reconstruction" rather than a "replanting." The reconstruction involved the church relocating and renaming itself the "San Francisco Church of Christ." The church's evangelists and women's counselors were stripped of their titles and demoted to interns so that "when they are appointed in the future, they will be recognized in Boston as well as in our church plantings, such as in Bombay or New York."

Other Boston-Affiliated Churches

A number of churches which were started through the influence of the Crossroads Church of Christ have since become a part of the Boston organization. In the August 30, 1987, Boston bulletin Kip McKean states that "San Diego and Denver must also be considered pillar churches and we praise God for the close discipling relationship that the leadership in Boston has been asked to have with the leaderships of these congregations."

Statements in the July 26, 1987, bulletin revealed the association of eight Southeastern "Crossroads" churches with Boston. Interviews with numerous churches and statements in the bulletin of the Chicago Church of Christ have revealed that many other churches also consider themselves part of the Boston Movement. It is unclear whether Boston exerts direct control over all of these churches. Yet these churches indicate a desire to be identified with the Boston discipling movement.

The following churches were not planted, "re-planted," or "reconstructed" by Boston, yet are under Boston's influence:

Mission Church of Christ in San Diego

The Mission church was heavily influenced by the coming of Andy and Rita Lindo in 1979. Many of their staff members were trained in the Boulder Church of Christ. The Mission church baptized close to 800 people from 1982 through 1986. The church is being discipled by Boston and is discipling the churches in Phoenix and Albuquerque.

Mt. Vista Church of Christ in Albuquerque

The Mt. Vista church began in 1984 without outside support. The church had a total of 70 baptisms and 50 members as of the end of 1986.

East Valley Church of Christ in Phoenix

The East Valley Church began in December 1984. The church experienced close to 200 baptisms in 1985 and 1986. Its membership at the end of 1986 stood at 260.

Denver Church of Christ

The Denver church was planted by the Crossroads Church of Christ (Gainesville, Florida) in May of 1986. By the end of 1986, 41 had been baptized.

Central Church of Christ in Huntsville, Alabama

University Church of Christ in Tallahassee, Florida

Crossroads Church of Christ in Gainesville, Florida

University Boulevard Church of Christ in Orlando, Florida

Westside Church of Christ in Ft. Lauderdale, Florida

Shandon Church of Christ in Columbia, South Carolina

Northview Church of Christ in Charlotte, North Carolina

Cornerstone Church of Christ in Champaign, Illinois

Gateway Church of Christ in Cincinnati

Lakeview Church of Christ in Milwaukee

Landmark Church of Christ in Indianapolis

CHAPTER 12

PILLAR CHURCHES AND FUTURE CHURCH PLANTINGS

The following information was derived primarily from the August 30, 1987, bulletin of the Boston Church of Christ. According to this bulletin, there are a total of 27 present and future "pillar churches." These churches each have supervision over a specific territory. That territory is named after the church's name.

Boston Church of Christ—Global

The Boston church is not listed as a "pillar church." Clearly, the Boston church is at the top of the pyramid and thus does not belong at the first level below the top.

The Boston church is not listed as a "pillar church." Clearly, the Boston church is at the top of the pyramid and thus does not belong at the first level below the top. As of August 1987 Boston had planted or taken control of seven domestic pillar churches and six foreign pillar churches. Future pillar churches to be planted directly from Boston include: Mexico City (1987), Buenos Aires (1988), Hong Kong (1988), Los Angeles, Miami, Washington, D.C., Munich (1988), Tokyo (1988), and Milan (1989). Thus, a total of 22 out of the 27 pillar churches are or will be direct Boston daughter churches, Boston has also targeted teams for Amsterdam, Athens, Cairo, Dublin, Lagos, Port-au-Prince, and Taipei.

Chicago—United States (particularly Midwest)

Chicago has planted a church in Minneapolis-St. Paul and replanted a church in St. Louis. Future targets include Philadelphia, Seattle, Dallas, Detroit, Portland, and Baltimore.

Atlanta—Southeastern United States

The Atlanta church has two roles: to plant churches in its territory and to "service the struggling discipling ministries in this region." Future plantings include "The Research Triangle," North Carolina; Knoxville, Tennessee; Lexington, Kentucky; Little Rock, Arkansas; Jacksonville, Florida; New Orleans; Norfolk, Virginia; Huntington, West Virginia; and Jackson, Mississippi.

San Diego—Southwestern United States

The Mission church in San Diego is responsible for California, Arizona, New Mexico, and Texas. The Mission church is already supervising churches in Phoenix and Albuquerque. Future targets include Houston and Orange County, California.

Denver—Western United States

This church was originally established by the Crossroads Church of Christ in 1986. Led by evangelist Marty Wooten, Denver plans to establish new churches throughout its territory and "striving to help some of the smaller discipling ministries in this part of the country as well."

Providence—Northeastern United States

The Providence church became separate from the Boston church in June 1985. Targets include Hartford, Connecticut, and Buffalo, New York.

Los Angeles—Pacific Rim

The Los Angeles church will be planted from Boston in 1988.

Washington, D.C.—unidentified territory

This church will be planted by the Boston church.

Miami—unidentified territory

This church will be planted by the Boston church.

San Francisco—Asia

Targets are Manila, Bangkok, and Seoul.

New York—Brazil, Africa, Portugal

The New York City church planted a church in São Paulo, Brazil, in June 1987. Future targets are New Brunswick, Delhi, Nairobi, and Lisbon.

London—Great Britain, Africa, Asia, Australia

The Central London church planted a church in Sydney, Australia, in January 1987. The London church has plans to send teams to Singapore, Bangalore, Manchester, Edinburgh, and Birmingham. According to the Boston bulletin, London will assist Boston in planting a church in Lagos, Nigeria.

Toronto—Canada

The Central Toronto church bears responsibility for planting churches throughout Canada. The church intends to plant churches in Vancouver and Montreal.

Mexico City—Central America and South America (northern)

The Mexico City church began in October 1987. Already, the Boston leadership has announced the future targets and "lead evangelists" of new teams. The targets are Guatemala City; San Jose, Costa Rica; Panama City; Tegucigalpa, Honduras; Santo Domingo, Dominican Republic; Caracas, Venezuela; and Bogotá, Colombia.

Buenos Aires—South America (western and southern)

Led by Martin Bentley, the Buenos Aires church is scheduled to begin in January 1988. The church has plans to establish churches in Quito, Ecuador; Lima, Peru; La Paz, Bolivia; Asunción, Paraguay; Montevideo, Uruguay; and Santiago, Chile.

São Paulo—Brazil and Portugal

This is one of five pillar churches not planted directly by Boston. The New York City church commissioned Mike Taliaferro to lead the São Paulo church. Targets from São Paulo include Rio de Janeiro and Lisbon.

Paris—French-Speaking Europe and Africa, and Poland

Tom Turnbull is the lead evangelist for this church planted by Boston in 1986. Future targets from Paris are Brussels, Belgium; Kinshasha, Zaire; and cities throughout France.

Stockholm—Scandinavia

Under the guidance of evangelist Andy Fleming, the Stockholm church has targets in Oslo, Norway; Copenhagen, Denmark; Helsinki, Finland; and Reykjavik, Iceland.

Helsinki—Finland and the Soviet Union

The Helsinki church will be planted by the Stockholm church in 1988. The Helsinki church will send its first team to Leningrad.

Milan—Italy and surrounding islands

Boston plans to plant the Milan church in 1989, with Bob Tranchell as the "team director." The Milan church will send teams to Rome, Bologna, and Palermo.

Munich—West Germany, Switzerland, Austria, Eastern Europe, and Istanbul

Boston will send a team led by Tom Marks, Henning Droeger, and Grant Henley to plant the Munich church in 1988. Targets include West Berlin and Vienna.

Vienna—Slavic Nations

Grant Henley is slated to plant this church from the Munich church. The Vienna church will be responsible for targeting Yugoslavia, Romania, Albana, Hungary, Bulgaria, and parts of the Soviet Union.

Bombay—India, Pakistan, Sri Lanka, Middle East

Planted by Boston in January of 1987, the Bombay church plans to coordinate its efforts to reach the surrounding area with the London and New York churches. Firm targets are Calcutta and Madras.

Tokyo—Japan, Okinawa

George Gurganus and Steve Shoff lead the Tokyo team as members study the language. The church will be planted in 1988 with Frank Kim as lead evangelist.

Hong Kong—China

Boston has set January 1988 as the starting date for the Hong Kong church. Led by Scott Green, this church will eventually attempt to plant churches in the key cities of mainland China.

Singapore—Malaysia, Indonesia

The London church is scheduled to plant a church in Singapore in 1988. The team's evangelists are James Lloyd and Daniel Eng.

Sydney—Australia, South Pacific

The London church planted the Sydney church in

January 1987. Future targets from Sydney include Melbourne and Auckland.

Kingston—Caribbean

Boston "replanted" this Jamaican congregation in January 1987. Under Boston's influence, the Kingston church has targeted Nassau, Bridgetown, and Port of Spain.

CHAPTER

13

BOSTON CHURCHES COUNTRY BY COUNTRY

The following is a list of all the known churches that are affiliated with the Boston movement and all of their future targets. Each church and target planting are listed as follows:

City of church (name of church, if different);
date of beginning;
church that planted this one.

North America

United States

Boston; June 1979, started by Kip McKean.
Chicago; June 1982; Boston.
New York City; June 1983; Boston.
Providence; June 1985; Boston.
Minneapolis (Twin Cities); January 1987; Chicago.
St. Louis; August 1987; "replanted" by Chicago.
Atlanta; August 1987; split from Atlanta Highlands and taken over by Boston.
San Francisco; September 1987; "reconstructed" by Boston.

The following churches were not planted directly by Boston, but are under Boston's influence:

San Diego (Mission), in 1987 began being discipled by Boston.
Albuquerque (Mt. Vista), in 1987 began being discipled by Mission church.

Phoenix (East Valley), in 1987 began being discipled by Mission church.
Denver, in 1987 began being discipled by Boston.
Huntsville, Alabama (Central)
Tallahassee, Florida (University)
Gainesville, Florida (Crossroads)
Orlando, Florida (University Boulevard)
Ft. Lauderdale, Florida (Westside)
Columbia, South Carolina (Shandon)
Charlotte, North Carolina (Northview)
Champaign, Illinois (Cornerstone)
Cincinnati (Gateway)
Milwaukee (Lakeview)
Indianapolis (Landmark)

Future Targets
Los Angeles; 1988; Boston
Miami; 1988; Boston
Washington, D.C.; 1988; Boston
Philadelphia; Chicago
Seattle; Chicago
Dallas; Chicago
Detroit; Chicago
Portland; Chicago
Baltimore; Chicago
"The Research Triangle," North Carolina; Atlanta
Knoxville, Tennessee; Atlanta
Lexington, Kentucky; Atlanta
Little Rock, Arkansas; Atlanta
Jacksonville, Florida; Atlanta
New Orleans; Atlanta
Norfolk, Virginia; Atlanta
Huntington, West Virginia; Atlanta
Jackson, Mississippi; Atlanta
Houston; San Diego (Mission)
Orange County, California; San Diego (Mission)
Hartford, Connecticut; Providence
Buffalo, New York; Providence

Canada

Toronto (Central Toronto); 1985; Boston

Future Targets
Vancouver; Toronto
Montreal; Toronto
New Brunswick; New York

Latin America and Carribean

Northern Latin America

Mexico City; 1987; Boston

Future Targets (City; Church Planter)
Guatemala City; Mexico City
San Jose, Costa Rica; Mexico City
Panama City; Mexico City
Tegucigalpa, Honduras; Mexico City
Santo Domingo, Dominican Republic; Mexico City
Caracas, Venezuela; Mexico City
Bogotá, Colombia; Mexico City

Western and Southern Latin America

Buenos Aires; 1988; Boston

Future Targets
Quito, Ecuador; Buenos Aires
Lima, Peru; Buenos Aires
La Paz, Bolivia; Buenos Aires
Asunción, Paraguay; Buenos Aires
Montevideo, Uruguay; Buenos Aires
Santiago, Chile; Buenos Aires

Brazil

São Paulo; 1987; New York City

Future Targets
Rio de Janeiro; São Paulo

Carribean

Kingston, Jamaica; 1987; "replanted" by Boston

Future Targets
Nassau, Bahamas; Kingston
Bridgetown, Barbados; Kingston
Port of Spain, Trinidad; Kingston
Port-au-Prince, Haiti; Boston

Europe

Great Britain and Ireland

London; 1982; Boston

Future Targets
Manchester; London
Birmingham; London
Edinburgh; London
Dublin; Boston

Western Europe

Paris; 1986; Boston

Future Targets
Brussels, Belgium; Paris
Amsterdam, Holland; Boston
Lisbon; New York and São Paulo, Brazil

Scandinavia

Stockholm; 1986; Boston

Future Targets
Helsinki, Finland; 1988; Stockholm
Oslo, Norway; Stockholm
Copenhagen, Denmark; Stockholm
Reykjavik, Iceland; Stockholm

Italy and Greece
Future Targets
Milan; 1989; Boston
Rome; Milan
Bologna; Milan
Palermo; Milan
Athens; Boston

Central and Eastern Europe
Future Targets
Munich, West Germany; 1988; Boston
West Berlin; Munich
Istanbul, Turkey; West Berlin
Vienna; Munich
Yugoslavia; Vienna
Romania; Vienna
Albania; Vienna
Hungary; Vienna
Bulgaria; Vienna
Soviet Union; Vienna
Leningrad, Soviet Union; Helsinki, Finland

Africa

Johannesburg, South Africa; 1986; Boston

Future Targets
Lagos, Nigeria; Boston and London
Cairo, Egypt; Boston
Nairobi, Kenya; New York
Kinshasha, Zaire; Paris

Asia and South Pacific

India and Middle East
Bombay; 1987; Boston

Future Targets
Calcutta; Bombay
Madras; Bombay
Delhi; New York
Pakistan; Bombay
Sri Lanka; Bombay

Far East
Hong Kong; 1988; Boston
Tokyo; 1988; Boston

Future Targets
Taipai, Taiwan; Boston
Manila, Philippines; San Francisco
Bangkok, Thailand; San Francisco
Seoul, South Korea; San Francisco
Singapore; 1988; London
Bangalore; London
Mainland China; Hong Kong

Australia and New Zealand
Sydney; 1987; London

Future Targets
Melbourne, Australia; Sydney
Auckland, New Zealand; Sydney

CHAPTER

14

BOSTON AND STATISTICS

Most, if not all, of the interest in the Boston methodology stems from their great numerical growth. Few are particularly impressed by their works righteousness theology, rigidly authoritarian structure, or arrogant attitudes. The only merit and attractiveness in the system is the numerical growth. It is appropriate, therefore, to look objectively at some statistics concerning that growth.

Staff Numbers

One key indicator used by church growth statisticians is the staff-to-member ratio. As of October 1987 the Boston Church of Christ had approximately 3000 in Sunday morning attendance. The total membership numbered about 2500. The Boston full-time payroll includes the following people: 2 full-time elders, 5 evangelists, 42 missionaries (not in Boston), 54 interns or other leaders, and 6 office personnel. Not counting the office staff and missionaries, Boston's effective ministerial staff numbers 61. The ratio of staff to members then is 1 to 40. Most of these staff members are engaged in full-time evangelism. A church of 400 with an equivalent ratio would have 10 full-time evangelists.

The staff-to-baptism ratio at Boston is 1 to 16. This

means that on average each evangelist or intern converts one person every 3 weeks.

These ratios are much the same throughout the Boston daughter churches. In Chicago there are 23 evangelists and interns on payroll. With an estimated membership of 850, the staff-to-member ratio is 1 to 37. The staff-to-baptism ratio is 1 to 17.

The growth of the Boston Movement churches is no great mystery. It is a direct result of the large number of evangelists and interns who are evangelizing full-time. That manpower is made possible largely because the Boston Movement churches do not own facilities. The money which most churches spend on purchasing a church building is spent on supporting evangelists.

The growth of the Boston Movement churches is no great mystery. It is a direct result of the large number of evangelists and interns who are evangelizing full-time.

Attrition Ratio

A few years ago, Boston boasted that they retained 95% of their converts. After 8 years in existence, however, the facts do not support those claims. Between June of 1979 and October of 1987 the Boston church baptized approximately 4200 persons. The most reliable indicator of Boston's membership is the Wednesday attendance. In the fall of 1987 the Wednesday attendance was at about 2700. This leaves a difference of 1500 or 35% of the baptisms that are not current members.

Of course an allowance should be made for those who left on mission teams or moved to different cities. We were not able to obtain that number from Boston. However, the number of those who left should be balanced by those who moved to Boston and placed membership. For example, the Boston bulletins indicate that in 1986 over 120 individuals placed membership at the Boston church. Therefore, the 65% retention estimate is probably accurate.

Even a 65% retention rate is better than most churches are able to achieve. A hidden factor must also be considered. Boston makes new converts so quickly that the dropouts of yesterday are overshadowed by the converts of today. As the Boston growth rate slows, the true dropout rate will become clear.

APPENDIX

by Flavil R. Yeakley, Jr.

The purpose of this appendix is to present the statistical details that support the claims made in Chapter 2. Several statistical tables are presented at the back of this appendix. This discussion is intended as an explanation of those tables.

Table 1 shows the type distribution in the study of the Boston Church of Christ. Type tables are displayed with the introverts in the top two rows and the extraverts in the bottom two rows. The eight sensing types are shown in the two columns on the left with the eight intuitive types in the two columns on the right. The two outer columns contain the eight thinking types and the two inner columns contain the eight feeling types. The eight judging types are displayed in the top and bottom rows while the eight perceiving types are in the two middle rows. Results are shown separately for males and females because of differences on the thinking-feeling scale. Approximately 60% of males prefer thinking judgment and only 40% prefer feeling judgment, but 60% of females prefer feeling judgment and only 40% prefer thinking judgment. The three rows in each cell represent outcomes on the three different forms of the MBTI.

Consider the ISTJ cell in the upper left corner as an example. Here is what the figures mean. When answering the questions on the MBTI the way they think they would have answered them before their conversion (or five years ago for the few who had been members that long), 16.49% of the males and 11.68% of the females came out ISTJ, thus indicating preferences for introversion, sensing, thinking, and judging. However, when they answered the questions indicating present preferences, only 8.46% of the males and 6.69% of the females came out ISTJ. Furthermore, when they answered the questions on the MBTI the way they think they will answer them after five more years of discipling, even fewer came out ISTJ—only 1.32% of the males and 1.30% of the females.

If you examine all 16 cells in Table 1, you will find that 10 of the psychological types show a steady decline from past to present to future outcomes. Three of the types—ISFJs, INFJs, and male ENTJs—show the largest percentages in the present outcome. These appear to be transitional types. The changes people are making move them into these types on their way to becoming something else. Three types—ESTJ, ESFJ, and ENFJ—show a steady increase from past to present to future outcomes. The most popular type is ESFJ with 54.23% of the males and 53.48% of the females indicating that type preference when answering the MBTI questions the way they think they will after five more years of discipling. The next most popular type is ESTJ with 20.37% of the males and 23.04% of the females indicating that as their future preference. The only other popular type is ENFJ with 14.81% of the males and 12.17% of the females indicating that future preference.

Table 2 shows the deviations from a base population in this study. The purpose of this comparison was to see which of the three distributions came closest to population norms. Since most of the members of the Boston Church of Christ are college students or college graduates, they were compared with a sample of college students and college graduates who have taken the MBTI. Each of the percentages in Table 1 was compared with a corresponding percentage in the base population. What is shown in Table 2 are the percentage point differences in the two figures. The mean percentage point deviation for the total sample was closest to population norms when members of the congregation answered the MBTI questions the way they think they would have answered them before their conversion (or five years ago for the few who had been members that long). The present outcome showed a greater mean deviation. The future outcome showed a much greater deviation from population norms.

Table 3 is a selection ratio type table showing the ratio of the percent of each type among church members to the percent of that type in the base population. A ratio of 1.00 would indicate a perfect match with exactly as many of that type in the sample as would be expected based on population norms. A ratio of 2.00 would indicate that the sample had twice as many of that type as would be expected on the basis of population norms. A ratio of 0.50 would indicate that the sample had only half as many of that type as would be expected on the basis of population norms. Many of the cells have significant under-representations in the future outcomes. The cells with the significant over-representations in the future outcomes are ESTJ, ESFJ, and ENFJ. There were more than eight times as many male ESFJs and more than three times as many female ESFJs as would be expected based on population norms.

The significance levels indicate how confident one can be that the observed differences do not result from chance and would be observed again in repeated samples. At the .05 level, there is only a 5% probability that the observed pattern resulted simple from chance. At the .01 level, there is only a 1% probability of such error and thus one can be more confident. At the .001 level, there is only one chance in 1,000 of such error and thus one can be still more confident. For any readers who are not familiar with statistics, significance levels in this kind of study are usually based on a statistic known as Chi Square. When some of the cells are empty or have very small numbers, it is necessary to use an alternative statistic known as Fisher's Exact Probability.

Table 4 is another selection ratio type table. This time, however, the comparison is not with population norms. Since the past distribution in this study came closest to population norms, that was taken as the best estimate of true type in the congregation. In Table 4, the present and future distributions are compared with the past distribution. What this table shows is that the changes in psychological type observed in the study of the Boston Church of Christ are statistically significant. The past-to-present changes are significant, but the past-to-future changes are highly significant.

Table 5 summarizes the changes on the four MBTI scales. Notice how the percentages change from past to present to future outcomes. Notice also how many of the members of the Boston Church of Christ show a future preference for extraversion, sensing, feeling, and judging.

Table 6 shows the past-to-future MBTI scale changes by type. The 16 types are listed in the left column following the usual type table order. The second column shows the number who indicated each type preference when they answered the questions the way they would have before conversion. The next columns show the percent and the actual number who had no past-future changes, then those who had one, two, three, or four changes. The column on the right shows the mean number of scale changes for each type. The figures across the bottom show the percent and the actual number who had no changes, one, two, three, or four changes, and the mean number of scale changes for the entire sample. What this shows is that the average member of the Boston Church of Christ changed on at least two of the MBTI scales. Only 6.83% had no past-future changes; 19.64% had one; 34.97% had two; 26.35% had three; and 12.22% had four and thus experienced a total reversal of type.

Table 7 shows the past-future scale changes by

preference. The figures on the left show the percent and the actual number who started with each preference. The figures in the middle show how many of those remained unchanged. The figures on the right show how many changed. What this shows is that those who started with preferences for extraversion, sensing, feeling, and judging tended to remain unchanged, but those who started with the opposite preferences tended to change.

Table 8 shows the past-future changes by preference. The mean number of scale changes was less for those who started with preferences for extraversion, sensing, feeling, and judging that it was for those who started with preferences for introversion, intuition, thinking, and perceiving.

Table 9 shows the past-future changes by combinations of preferences. In each of the sets of four, one combination includes two of the ESFJ preferences, two combinations include one of the ESFJ preferences, and the other combination does not include any of the ESFJ preferences. In each of the five sets, the combination that includes two of the ESFJ preferences shows the least change and the combination that does not include any of the ESFJ preferences shows the greatest change.

Table 10 shows the past-future changes by type. On the left side of this table, the 16 types are arranged in order from the type that showed the least change (ESFJ) to the type that showed the greatest change (INTP). The ranking at the right side of this table is based on differences from ESFJ. ESFJs, of course, have zero difference points and INTPs have four. There is a Spearman rho rank order correlation of .91 between these two ranking and that correlation is significant at the .001 level.

Tables 5 through 10 all make the same basic point: the group dynamics in the Boston Church of Christ operate to influence a movement away from introversion, intuition, thinking, and perceiving with a strong movement toward extraversion, sensing, feeling, and judging.

Keep in mind that these statistical tables do not prove that any individual is going to experience the psychological problems associated with falsification of psychological type. The focus of this research was not on any individual, but rather on the overall pattern observed in the group. This pattern, however, clearly indicates a potential danger for the individuals subjected to this kind of influence. Those who are already ESFJs when they come to the Boston Church of Christ are likely to fit in quite well and not feel much of the pressure toward conformity that others feel. The greater the difference between a person's true type and the ESFJ model, the more likely that person is to feel the pressure toward conformity. Those who come to the Boston church as INTPs are in the greatest danger.

TABLE 1
TYPE DISTRIBUTION

	ISTJ		ISFJ		INFJ		INTJ	
	male	female	male	female	male	female	male	female
Past	16.49%	11.68%	4.12%	8.28%	1.55%	1.70%	2.06%	1.70%
Present	8.46%	6.69%	15.17%	17.36%	3.48%	2.51%	1.99%	1.05%
Future	1.32%	1.30%	3.17%	1.52%	0.26%	0.65%	0.00%	0.00%
	ISTP		**ISFP**		**INFP**		**INTP**	
	male	female	male	female	male	female	male	female
Past	13.92%	11.25%	11.60%	9.98%	9.28%	9.98%	8.25%	7.22%
Present	1.49%	1.67%	5.47%	3.97%	3.73%	2.72%	0.50%	0.42%
Future	0.00%	0.43%	0.53%	0.22%	0.53%	0.22%	0.00%	0.22%
	ESTP		**ESFP**		**ENFP**		**ENTP**	
	male	female	male	female	male	female	male	female
Past	6.44%	6.58%	3.61%	8.07%	6.70%	9.13%	3.35%	3.82%
Present	1.99%	1.67%	3.48%	5.44%	2.74%	2.51%	0.50%	1.67%
Future	0.26%	0.65%	0.53%	1.30%	1.85%	1.30%	0.00%	0.43%
	ESTJ		**ESFJ**		**ENFJ**		**ENTJ**	
	male	female	male	female	male	female	male	female
Past	7.73%	4.67%	2.58%	5.10%	1.29%	0.64%	1.03%	0.21%
Present	15.92%	13.81%	26.37%	34.31%	4.73%	3.97%	3.98%	0.21%
Future	20.37%	23.04%	54.23%	53.48%	14.81%	12.17%	2.12%	3.14%

"Past Self" instructions: 378 males, 471 females
"Present Self" instructions: 402 males, 478 females
"Future Self" instructions: 388 males, 460 females
Number who completed all three forms: 835

TABLE 2
DEVIATIONS FROM BASE POPULATION
(percentage points)

	ISTJ		ISFJ		INFJ		INTJ	
	male	female	male	female	male	female	male	female
Past	5.92	5.66	−2.12	−3.90	−1.37	−2.08	−2.23	−0.21
Present	−2.11	0.67	8.93	5.18	0.56	−1.27	−2.30	−0.86
Future	−9.25	−4.72	−3.07	−10.66	−2.66	−3.13	−4.29	−1.91

	ISTP		ISFP		INFP		INTP	
	male	female	male	female	male	female	male	female
Past	7.16	9.04	6.51	3.86	3.44	4.21	2.44	−5.27
Present	−5.27	−0.54	0.38	−2.15	−2.11	−3.05	−5.31	−1.53
Future	−6.76	−1.78	−4.56	−5.90	−5.31	−5.55	−5.81	−1.73

	ESTP		ESFP		ENFP		ENTP	
	male	female	male	female	male	female	male	female
Past	0.00	−4.02	−1.78	−0.52	−0.74	−3.21	−2.85	0.76
Present	−4.45	−0.89	−1.91	−3.15	−4.70	−9.83	−5.70	−1.39
Future	−6.18	−1.91	−4.86	−7.29	−5.55	−11.04	−6.20	−2.63

	ESFJ		ESFJ		ENFJ		ENTJ	
	male	female	male	female	male	female	male	female
Past	−3.47	−2.86	−4.04	−11.35	−2.40	−6.24	−4.39	−2.41
Present	4.72	6.28	19.75	17.86	−1.04	−2.91	−1.44	−2.44
Future	9.17	15.51	48.01	37.03	11.12	5.29	−3.30	−0.39

Base Population: 5,632 male and 9,616 female college students
Church Members—
"Past Self" instructions: 378 males, 471 females
"Present Self" instructions: 402 males, 478 females
"Future Self" instructions: 388 males, 460 females
Number who completed all three forms: 835

Mean percentage point devitions from base population:

	male	female	combined
Past	3.18	4.15	3.48
Present	4.42	3.75	4.06
Future	8.51	7.28	7.84

TABLE 3

SELECTION RATIO TYPE TABLE

Ratio of Percent of Type among Church Members to Percent of Type in Base Population

	ISTJ		ISFJ		INFJ		INTJ	
	male	female	male	female	male	female	male	female
Past	1.56*	1.94*	.66	.68#	.53	.45"	.48"	.89
Present	.80	1.11	2.42*	1.42*	1.19	.66	.46"	.55
Future	.12*	.22*	.51"	.12*	.09#	.17*	.00*	.00#

	ISTP		ISFP		INFP		INTP	
	male	female	male	female	male	female	male	female
Past	2.06*	5.08*	2.28*	1.63*	1.59#	1.73*	1.42"	3.71*
Present	.22*	.76	1.07	.65	.64	.47#	.09*	.22"
Future	.00*	.20"	.10*	.04*	.09*	.04*	.00*	.11#

	ESTP		ESFP		ENFP		ENTP	
	male	female	male	female	male	female	male	female
Past	1.00	2.57*	.67	.94	.90	.74"	.54"	1.25
Present	.31*	.65	.65	.64"	.37*	.20*	.08*	.55
Future	.04*	.25"	.10*	.15*	.25*	.11*	.00*	.14#

	ESTJ		ESFJ		ENFJ		ENTJ	
	male	female	male	female	male	female	male	female
Past	.69"	.62"	.39#	.31*	.35"	.09*	.19*	.07*
Present	1.42#	1.83*	4.00*	2.12*	1.28	.58"	.74	.07*
Future	1.81*	3.06*	8.23*	3.30*	4.01*	1.77*	.39#	1.07

Note Concerning Symbols Following the Selection Ratios:

" = significance at the .05 level, Chi Square greater than 3.8
= significance at the .01 level, Chi Square greater than 6.6
* = significance at the .001 level, Chi Square greater than 10.8
Underscore indicates Fisher's Exact Probability used instead of Chi Square

TABLE 4

SELECTION RATIO TYPE TABLE COMPARING PRESENT AND FUTURE DISTRIBUTIONS WITH PAST DISTRIBUTION

	ISTJ		ISFJ		INFJ		INTJ	
	male	female	male	female	male	female	male	female
Present	.51*	.57#	3.68*	2.10*	2.25	1.48	.97	.62
Future	.08*	.11*	.77	.18*	.17	.38	.00#	.00*

	ISTP		ISFP		INFP		INTP	
	male	female	male	female	male	female	male	female
Present	.11*	.15*	.47#	.40*	.40#	.27*	.06*	.06*
Future	.00*	.04*	.05*	.02*	.06*	.02*	.00*	.03*

	ESTP		ESFP		ENFP		ENTP	
	male	female	male	female	male	female	male	female
Present	.31#	.25*	.97	.67	.41#	.27*	.15#	.44"
Future	.04*	.10*	.15#	.16*	.28*	.14*	.00*	.11*

	ESTJ		ESFJ		ENFJ		ENTJ	
	male	female	male	female	male	female	male	female
Present	2.06*	2.96*	10.23*	6.73*	3.67#	6.24*	3.86"	.99
Future	2.63*	4.93*	21.04*	10.50*	11.50*	19.11*	2.05	14.33*

Note Concerning Symbols Following the Selection Ratios:

" = significance at the .05 level, Chi Square greater than 3.8

= significance at the .01 level, Chi Square greater than 6.6

* = significance at the .001 level, Chi Square greater than 10.8

Underscore indicates Fisher's Exact Probability used instead of Chi Square

TABLE 5

SUMMARY OF CHANGES ON THE FOUR MBTI SCALES

	Past		Present		Future	
	male	female	male	female	male	female
Extraversion	33%	38%	60%	64%	94%	95%
Introversion	67%	62%	40%	36%	6%	5%
Sensing	66%	66%	78%	85%	80%	82%
Intuition	34%	34%	22%	15%	20%	18%
Thinking	59%	47%	35%	27%	24%	29%
Feeling	41%	53%	65%	73%	76%	71%
Judging	37%	34%	80%	80%	96%	95%
Perceiving	63%	66%	20%	20%	4%	5%

TABLE 6

PAST-FUTURE MBTI SCALE CHANGES BY TYPE

		Number of Past-Future Changes on the MBTI Scales										
		None		One		Two		Three		Four		
Type	N	%	N	%	N	%	N	%	N	%	N	Mean
ISTJ	115	2.61	3	21.74	25	51.30	59	20.87	24	3.48	4	2.01
ISFJ	53	11.32	6	50.94	27	30.19	16	7.55	4	0.00	0	1.34
INFJ	14	0.00	0	14.29	2	64.29	9	21.42	3	0.00	0	2.07
INTJ	16	0.00	0	6.25	1	37.50	6	56.25	9	0.00	0	2.50
ISTP	100	0.00	0	3.00	3	21.00	21	64.00	64	12.00	12	2.85
ISFP	90	2.22	2	5.55	5	56.67	51	13.33	12	22.22	20	2.48
INFP	85	1.18	1	3.53	3	20.00	17	43.53	37	31.77	27	3.01
INTP	63	0.00	0	1.59	1	3.17	2	33.33	21	61.90	39	3.55
ESTP	57	1.75	1	26.32	15	59.65	34	12.28	7	0.00	0	1.82
ESFP	49	4.08	2	57.14	28	30.61	15	8.16	4	0.00	0	1.37
ENFP	67	4.48	3	8.96	6	59.70	40	26.87	18	0.00	0	2.03
ENTP	30	3.33	1	13.33	4	26.67	8	56.67	17	0.00	0	2.37
ESTJ	49	22.45	11	55.10	27	22.45	11	0.00	0	0.00	0	1.00
ESFJ	34	70.59	24	26.47	9	2.94	1	0.00	0	0.00	0	0.32
ENFJ	7	28.57	2	57.14	4	14.29	1	0.00	0	0.00	0	0.86
ENTJ	6	16.67	1	66.67	4	16.67	1	0.00	0	0.00	0	1.17
Totals	835		57		164		292		220		102	2.18
Percent of total		6.83 No Changes		19.64 One Change		34.97 Two Changes		26.35 Three Changes		12.22 Four Changes		

TABLE 7
PAST-FUTURE MBTI SCALE CHANGES BY PREFERENCE

Preference	%	N	Remaining Unchanged %	N	Changing %	N
Extraversion	35.81	299	96.66	289	3.34	10
Introversion	64.19	536	5.41	29	94.59	507
Sensing	65.39	546	82.23	449	17.77	97
Intuition	34.61	289	22.15	64	77.85	225
Thinking	52.22	436	25.69	112	74.31	324
Feeling	47.78	399	72.43	289	27.57	110
Judgment	35.21	294	96.94	285	3.06	9
Perception	64.79	541	5.18	28	94.82	513

TABLE 8
PAST-FUTURE CHANGES BY PREFERENCE

Scale	N	Mean Changes
E	299	1.51
I	536	2.53
S	547	1.90
N	288	2.67
T	436	2.31
F	399	2.01
J	294	1.51
P	541	2.52

TABLE 9
PAST-FUTURE CHANGES BY COMBINATIONS OF PREFERENCES

Scales	N	Mean Changes
IJ	198	1.87
IP	338	2.92
EP	203	1.86
EJ	96	0.76
ST	321	2.08
SF	226	1.65
NF	173	2.47
NT	115	2.97
SJ	251	1.44
SP	296	2.29
NP	245	2.80
NJ	43	1.91
TJ	186	1.76
TP	250	2.73
FP	291	2.34
FJ	108	1.08
IN	178	3.08
EN	110	2.00
IS	358	2.26
ES	189	1.22

TABLE 10
PAST-FUTURE CHANGES BY TYPE
(a comparison of two rankings)

Type	N	Mean Changes	ranking based on differences from ESFJ
ESFJ	34	0.32	0
ENFJ	7	0.86	1
ESTJ	49	1.00	1
ENTJ	6	1.17	2
ISFJ	53	1.34	1
ESFP	49	1.37	1
ESTP	57	1.82	2
ISTJ	115	2.01	2
ENFP	67	2.03	2
INFJ	14	2.07	2
ENTP	30	2.37	3
ISFP	90	2.48	2
INTJ	16	2.50	3
ISTP	100	2.85	3
INFP	85	3.01	3
INTP	63	3.55	4

(Types rank ordered from least to most past-future change)

rho = .91 $p < .001$